Parametric Building Design Using Autodesk Maya

Ming Tang

First published 2014
by Routledge
2 Park Square, Milton Park, Abingdon, Oxon OX14 4RN

Simultaneously published in the USA and Canada
by Routledge
711 Third Avenue, New York, NY 10017

Routledge is an imprint of the Taylor & Francis Group, an informa business

© 2014 Ming Tang

The right of Ming Tang to be identified as author of this work has been asserted by him in accordance with sections 77 and 78 of the Copyright, Designs and Patents Act 1988.

All rights reserved. No part of this book may be reprinted or reproduced or utilised in any form or by any electronic, mechanical, or other means, now known or hereafter invented, including photocopying and recording, or in any information storage or retrieval system, without permission in writing from the publishers.

Trademark notice: Product or corporate names may be trademarks or registered trademarks, and are used only for identification and explanation without intent to infringe.

Every effort has been made to contact and acknowledge copyright owners. The publishers would be grateful to hear from any copyright holder who is not acknowledged here and will undertake to rectify any errors or omissions in future printings or editions of the book.

British Library Cataloguing in Publication Data
A catalogue record for this book is available from the British Library

Library of Congress Cataloging in Publication Data
Parametric Building Design using Autodesk Maya, Ming Tang.

ISBN: 978-0-415-64446-4 (hbk)
ISBN: 978-0-415-64447-1 (pbk)
ISBN: 978-1-315-81987-7 (ebk)

Typeset by Dihua Yang

Parametric Building Design Using Autodesk Maya

Due to its comprehensive tool-set and great potential for 3-D modeling, more and more architectural design and interior design firms are adapting Autodesk Maya and integrating it into their practice. There has been no book aimed at architects and designers who wish to harness the opportunities presented by this software, until now.....

The book promotes parametric design. It integrates the theoretical research of computational design and Maya nonlinear modeling techniques associated with simulation, animation, digital fabrication, and form-finding within 2-D & 3-D design. Readers will learn:

- How to use Maya polygon and NURBS modeling tools to create nonlinear procedural model.

- How to use Maya driver keys and relationship tools to generate parametrically negotiable solutions across various design professions.

- The design logic and generative processes, as well as the potential of parametric thinking as a resourceful tool for achieving diversity and complexity in form generation and fabrication.

- How to use Maya to prepare files for rapid prototyping and integrate Maya into various fabrication techniques such as laser cutting, CNC milling, and 3-D printing.

- How to simulate material properties and dynamic forces with Maya physics engine.

- How to use Maya skeleton system and animation tools to control complex architectural forms.

- How to create photo-realistic renderings with Maya lighting, material, and texture mapping. Using several real projects as examples, the book will go through the entire rendering process step by step.

- How to combine Maya with various CAD/BIM tools to create an efficient design pipeline.

- How to use Maya MEL script to create customized tools and interface.

The book includes case studies from Zaha Hadid Architects, Greg Lynn Form, Gage Clemenceau Architects, Tang & Yang Architects, as well as step by step exercises, demonstration projects, and crucially a fantastic online resource, which includes video tutorials, scripts, and Maya source files.

Ming Tang LEED AP, is an Assistant Professor at School of Architecture and Interior Design, University of Cincinnati. He is also the founding partner of Tang & Yang Architects, which has won design awards in China, Spain, Mexico, U.K. and United States, including the first prize of d3 Natural System, the first place of Cities with Soul, the first place of IAAC self-sufficient housing contest, and the first place of Chichen Itza lodge museum design.

homepage: http://ming3d.com

CONTENTS

Foreword	**7**
Preface	**11**
Acknowledgements	**13**
Chapter 1: Introduction	**15**
1.1 Parametric design in architecture	16
1.2 Computational and nonlinear thinking	17
1.3 Performance Based Design (PBD)	18
1.4 Using Autodesk Maya for parametric design	19
1.4.1 Case studies	19
1.4.2 Nonlinear modeling in Maya	36
1.4.3 Performance based design in Maya	37
1.5 Objective of the book	38
1.6 Tutorials	39
1.6.1 Tutorial: Basic Maya interface	39
1.6.2 Tutorial: Nonlinear modeling with Maya	40
1.6.3 Tutorial: 2-D pattern making in Maya	41
1.6.4 Tutorial: Polygon frames	43
Chapter 2. Maya modeling	**47**
2.1 Polygon modeling	48

2.2 NURBS model	49
2.3 Choosing the right modeling technique	50
2.4 Conversion between polygon model and NURBS model	52
2.5 Tutorials	53
2.5.1 Tutorial: Tessellation and iterative building skin	53
2.5.2 Tutorial: Parametric beam and roof	56
2.5.3 Tutorial: Deformation (NURBS + polygon)	59
Chapter 3: Parametric relationship	**63**
3.1 Morphing and blending	64
3.2 Tutorial: Hybrid house	67
3.3 Driven key	69
3.3.1 Driven key controlled morph	69
3.3.2 Attractor controlled morph	70
3.3.3 Case study: Folded paneling system	71
3.3.4 Tutorial: Adaptive skin	77
Chapter 4: Maya skeleton	**81**
4.1 Architectural application of Maya skeleton	82
4.2 Tutorials	88
4.2.1 Tutorial: Kinetic radial structure	88
4.2.2 Tutorial: Walking machine	90
Chapter 5: Simulation	**93**
5.1 Simulation for Performance Based Design and form seeking	94
5.2 Physics simulation as an artistic design approach	95
5.3 Maya dynamics simulation	96
5.4 Maya particle system and form making	97
5.5 Tutorials	104
5.5.1 Tutorial: nCloth for tensile structure - method 1	104

5.5.2 Tutorial: nCloth for tensile structure - method 2   105

5.5.3 Tutorial: Maya Hair and the tensile structure   106

Chapter 6: Visualization   **109**

6.1 Camera   111

6.1.1 Camera view   111

6.1.2 Camera lens   111

6. 2 Lighting   113

6.2.1 Light properties   113

6.2.2 Shadow   113

6.2.3 Light and vertex color   114

6.2.4 Tutorial: Bake Maya lighting into vertex color   116

6.3 Material   118

6.3.1 Shader and materials   118

6.3.2 Maya shader network   119

6.3.3 Procedural texture vs. bitmap texture   119

6.3.4 Map / channel   119

6.3.5 Color map / channel   119

6.3.6 Bump map / channel   119

6.3.7 Transparency map / channel   119

6.3.8 Reflection map / channel   121

6.3.9 Self-illumination map / channel   121

6.4 Special render nodes   121

6.4.1 Ambient occlusion   121

6.4.2 Soft edge shader   122

6.4.3 Ramp color   122

6.5 Projection   123

6.5.1 Projection types   123

6.5.2 Tutorial: Texture mapping — 126

6.5.3 Tutorial: Tri-planar projection — 127

6.5.4 Tutorial: Creating details with texture mapping — 128

6.5.5 Tutorial: Ambient occlusion rendering — 130

6.5.6 Tutorial: Reflection map and self-illumination material — 131

6. 6 Rendering — 132

6.6.1 Image composite — 135

6.6.2 Tutorial: Multiple layer rendering — 136

Chapter 7: Animation — **137**

7.1 Animation as visualization tool — 138

7.2 Animation as a modeling tool — 139

7.2.1 Animation of CV — 139

7.2.2 Deformation animation — 144

7.2.3 Animate the history nodes — 144

7.2.4 Animation through motion path — 144

7.2.5 Animation through parent / child relationship — 144

7.2.6 Animation through simulation — 145

7.3 Tutorials — 146

7.3.1 Tutorial: Keyframe animation — 146

7.3.2 Tutorial: Motion path animation — 147

7.3.3 Tutorial: Animation on object level and component level — 148

Chapter 8: Digital fabrication — **149**

8.1 CAD & CAM — 150

8.2. Laser cutting — 151

8.2.1 Laser cutting 2-D patterns — 151

8.2.2 Files for laser cutting — 152

8.2.3 Laser cutting for 3-D objects — 153

8.3 CNC	155
8.3.1 Tool path	155
8.4 3-D print	157
8.5 Case study	158
8.5.1 Mathmorph	158
8.5.2 Fractal imprint	160
8.6 Future of CAD and CAM	160
8.7 Tutorial: Tool path making	161
Chapter 9. Scripting	**163**
9.1 MEL Script	164
9.2 Tutorials	166
9.2.1 Tutorial: Super Extrude	166
9.2.2 Tutorial: Random weave	169
9.2.3 Tutorial: Image sampling	171
9.2.4 Tutorial: Zoning map for a digital city	173
Chapter 10. In and out	**181**
10.1 Transfer data across programs	182
10.2 Import data into Maya	182
10.3 Export data from Maya	182
10.4 Tutorials	185
10.4.1 Tutorial: From Revit to Maya	185
10.4.2 Tutorial: From Maya to Revit	187
10.4.3 Tutorial: Export geometry and vertex color from Maya to Rhino	188
Notes	**191**
Project credits	**197**
References	**199**
Index	**201**

Online materials:

Video tutorials, Maya example files, and MEL scripts are provided online at

http://ming3d.com/book/resource

Password: learningmaya

Software required:

The trial version of Autodesk Maya can be downloaded from Autodesk website. Qualified students may download student version of Maya from http://students.autodesk.com.

FOREWORD

If software had a sex appeal and a gender, Maya would definitely be a beautiful woman, a diva. One of those characters loved by many but also criticized by those who question her talent, yet always capable of fascinating people despite their prejudices. Like all beautiful women Maya has its air of mystery that can scare someone from trying to approach her, almost giving the feeling of being "not for everybody". This is particularly true when it comes to architecture since the use of Maya as a design research platform has been so far confined to few advanced university programmes around the world and even fewer international practices.

Although when we look back to the progresses made by our discipline in the last two decades in terms of spatial language and experimentation it is undeniable that this software, which was never created with architecture in mind, has been constantly among the platforms of choice for the most innovative researches and projects along the entire "digital era". As documented in Greg Lynn's book *Animate Form*, back in the in the late nineties, the most tangible legacy of the newborn "digital revolution" in architecture was the early experimentation that used Maya animation tools to create forms in motion. Fifteen years later we are still learning and exploring new features and possibilities to implement this package to create breakthrough architectural concepts.

That is what makes Maya so unique: the sense of constant discovery a designer feels when navigating the software interface not only for the number of instruments available but also because using any tool in Maya to design architecture is a creative choice on its own. In fact the key to developing a successful concept with Maya relies on the capability of the designer to critically reinvent, readapt and customize the extensive palette of possibilities offered by the software to fit their own design intent. Often the concept can fully coincide with this strategy in which case the final result can be really something unexpected and new, yet not random and uncontrolled as it comes from the logical coherence of the design process.

Maya is a form synthesizer, a generator of ideas that goes beyond any classification if compared to other traditional 3-D tools for architects. It is not a CAD but still it can produce fine NURBS surfaces with robust and highly interactive history-based tools, it is not a BIM but its node-based architecture allows one to define complex parametric relationships and behaviors, it is not just a 3-D sketch software but its implementation of Catmull-Clarke subdivision surfaces allows one to quickly design complex organic forms in no time. All you have to do is pressing the magic "3" button and a new world of possibilities will be disclosed to your eyes.

But the most interesting territory of exploration within Maya is definitely exploited by its simulation engines which are capable of virtually reproducing physical behaviors existing in nature. By feeding the design process with physically accurate tools not only can the designer achieve coherence and integration between the initial concept, its references, and the final design, but it is also possible to investigate form finding approaches, generative approaches, thus adding intelligence and performative criteria to the outcome.

Quite often though in order to get the most out of these tools it might be required to have a look under Maya's hood. In effect some attributes and node connections can only be performed via scripting using MEL (Maya Embedded Language). Luckily enough MEL is not very hard to learn and it is definitely worth it considering that it

is fully integrated within the interface to the point that Maya visualizes and keeps track of any command performed within the scene in MEL language. This way it is quite simple to get used to MEL syntax and writing scripts since there is no need to remember every single command.

All that said, I believe it is extremely difficult, if not impossible, to learn how to use Maya for architecture by reading any generic book written for character animators, special effects or CGI. That literature can only describe what the software was designed for and how artists can use it in cinema industry to produce those stunning special effects and 3-D movies we all know and enjoy watching.

As opposite learning Maya for architecture means going through the palimpsest of creative processes that students, researchers and avant-garde architects have built over the years , and once one has mastered the workflow and some tools it is also possible to variate or recombine them, or even invent brand new ones with their own logics. It is very much like learning jazz; you have got to play the best riff and solos if you want to be able to play your very own improvisation.

That is the reason why I welcome this book and I am really proud to be introducing it, because I strongly believe that the only way to effectively improve architectural research is by sharing knowledge and creativity.

Going back to the initial metaphor, I met this beautiful woman called Maya back in 2005 and since then I have never stopped being surprised and fascinated by what she is able to do when supported by a creative and critical mind. I have had the privilege of seeing some of the finest designers working with Maya and learned and experimented my personal workflows. After seven years her air of mystery remains intact for me, there are still many unknowns. Everyday I meet her and it is always a brand new story for me, with its incipit and its ending, hopefully a good one. All I can advise those designers who get lured by her beauty is not to be shy and enter her world with passion and commitment, since she will change their way of thinking about design forever.

Fulvio Wirz

Lead Architect, Zaha Hadid Architects

10

PREFACE

The only limit you have is your imagination.

In 1998, I was deeply impressed by the amazing short animation film *Bingo,* made by Maya program. This award-winning film demonstrated the great power of digital technology in the motion picture industry. Ever since then, Maya has played an essential role in the world of CGI and pushed the limits of digital technology. Over the past fifteen years, I have paid close attention to the evolution of Maya and applied this program through a series of projects with MIND Lab in Michigan State University, ICT in the University of South California, and Savannah College of Art and Design. Maya inspired me and freed my imagination with its infinite power. I am enthusiastic to see the rapid development of the program in recent years, especially the latest nucleus engine and simulation field. It is evident that Maya has expanded beyond being a tool merely for the motion picture industry, but also for other fields including architectural and interior design.

The essential challenge for me, as a designer and educator in the field of architectural design, is how to embrace this non architectural program and integrate it with my design flow. In the early 1990s, only a few architects were using Maya program. Greg Lynn is one of the pioneers who introduced computational methods into architectural design. His research on advanced modeling and animation has changed my mind-set in this field.

Since 2003, I have embraced Maya in several digital design and computation-related courses in the architectural and interior design program at University of Cincinnati and Savannah College of Art and Design. The software became a vehicle to introduce parametric design, digital fabrication, simulation, scripting, performance driven design, and nonlinear thinking. Much of my academic research has been shared through various books, journals, exhibitions, and presentations at ACSA, ACADIA, SIGGRPH, SIMAUD, and CAADRIA. After years of accumulating my research and teaching materials, it is necessary to organize them into a book and share the knowledge with the larger design community.

It is not my intention to write this book as a comprehensive introduction to various Maya tools, but rather to write an exploration of specific design processes from the architectural and interior design aspect. The book intends to explore the potential of Maya in the building design process, rather than the modeling process, with the goal of extending the knowledge of parametric design and seeking novel design solutions. The book is not a collection of end results with eye-candy renderings; it is a breakdown of the design process as simple steps that the reader can follow and execute. It also highlights the advantages of using Maya in the conceptual design stages and how to integrate Maya with other CAD programs.

By using this parametric design program, architects and designers are integrating digital computation with analytical design processes. These processes are emerging as a new direction in computational design and provide unprecedented methods for the exploration of forms, simulation of physical properties, and evaluation of building performance.

Ming Tang

ACKNOWLEDGEMENTS

Thanks go to Dihua Yang, Zhiliang Xiao, Fulvio Wirz, John Herridge, Nnamdi Elleh, Frank Biocca, Jonathon Anderson, Fran Ford, Laura Williamson, Greg Lynn Form, Gage Clemenceau Architects, Zaha Hadid Architects, as well as all of my colleagues and friends who have given me continuing support during my working process.

14

1 INTRODUCTION

INTRODUCTION

Parameter is a common term used to identify a characteristic, a feature, or a measurable factor that can help in defining a particular system.[1] In mathematics functions, a *parametric equation* defines the relation of parameters and variables. For instance, the following shows a simple math equation that defines a line with X and Y values. In this equation, X is a variable, while A and B are two parameters.

$$Y = AX + B$$

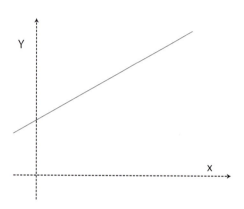

1.1 PARAMETRIC DESIGN IN ARCHITECTURE

Parametric design in architecture is a design approach that generates geometric solutions based on a family of related parameters. It emphasizes on the geometric relations between parameters and forms and uses variables and algorithms to quantify such geometric relations. For instance, designers can use 3-D software and apply parametric design methods to generate division points on a surface. Once the points have been defined, the surface is populated with a set of connecting triangles that have no overlap. This process leaves a triangulated surface determined by the number of division points. In architectural design, each triangle can be used to design a flat panel. A paneling system can thus be created and controlled through a few parameters, such as the number of divisions. The paneling system can possess a higher level of complexity by introducing new variables into the equation such as the size of openings to create perforated panels.

Parametric design software provides architects with a series of tools to evaluate ideas in the early design phase. One of the design challenges when designing with digital models is how to evaluate the relation between a form and its performance. For instance, the geometric shape of a sunshade will affect how it casts shadows and blocks sun light. When a digital sunshade model is constructed with a set of parameters, these parameters can be modified to design the sunshade to achieve certain performance. There is an emerging design method to analyze various performance-related parameters and optimize them according to predefined rules. Designers can use parametrically controlled variables to produce alternative solutions for comparison. This approach completely transforms the design process and allows for performance-driven design and simulation to be integrated into the design process.

Parametric design also extends the digital practice into the materialization and fabrication field. Through parametric methods, highly complex architectural forms can be digitally constructed and controlled by a set of parameters. Designers can parametrically modify the digital model and prepare it for fabrication, while simultaneously evaluating its performance based on environmental, structural, or other design constraints. The parametric method revitalizes the design world's interest in iterations because it offers greater variations through a set of controlled mathematical parameters. This file-to-factory process enables the information flow from representational format directly to the drawings for fabrication and construction.

1.2 COMPUTATIONAL AND NONLINEAR THINKING

This book describes various methods of using parametric techniques associated with architecture design. With a set of parameters and a series of operations, a parametric model provides opportunities for designers to revisit early design decisions or generate design alternatives without redoing all the subsequence operations. Parametrically negotiable solutions can be improved through this nonlinear procedure and can achieve diversity and complexity in form generation. It is the integration of the qualitative evaluation from human brain and the powerful computation capacity of software that offers greater potentials in the exploration of innovative design solutions. By using the nonlinear design pipeline, iterations are explored by defining a network of operation nodes and variables.

"The outcome of parametric design procedure surpasses traditional views of an optimized single solution that

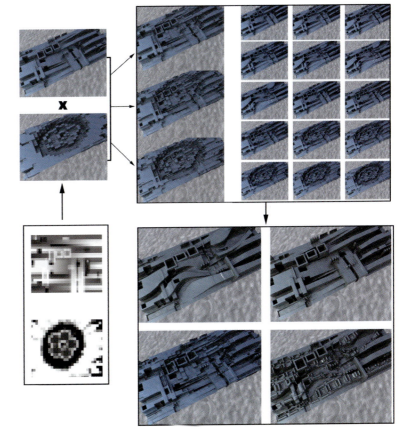

Geno Roof. In this roof modeling experiment, a prototype matrix was created to drive the deformation of a target geometry mesh. A large quantity of children roof surfaces was produced from each pair of roof parents. The first child was identical to parent A, while the last child was identical to parent B. Other children were the mixture of parent A and B with different weight combinations.

INTRODUCTION

travels down a linear pipeline—architect, engineer, contractor, and fabricator—to seek approval from various design professionals. The computation approach offers a non-linear process that contains parameters that perform actions based on the quantifiable relation in an open-end design loop." [2]

The gap between digital and physical realms is narrowing with the rapid development of digital fabrication technologies such as computer numerically controlled (CNC) mills, laser cutters, 3-D printers, and others. Designers can integrate various parameters, such as material property, tolerance, deformation, and cutting time, into the parametric equations and examinethe cost, structure, responsive performance, as well as other related information in digital format. This nonlinear procedure works as an interactive learning tool for construction prototyping and serves as an efficient way to transfer the end result of digital forms into full-scale manufactured parts.

1.3 PERFORMANCE BASED DESIGN (PBD)

Computation and nonlinear thinking promote performance-based design (PBD). "Powerful parametric tools provide both geometric modeling and analysis functions within a procedurally controlled network. The performance data, such as heat gain, stress, and solar radiation, can be easily quantified and defined to interact with other parameters." [3] Oxman describes it as design informed by internal evaluation. "Performance driven design is a process to create a system of parameters which can be verified, validated and evaluated with facts. Supported by the modeling and simulations, Performance Based Design (PBD) uses evidence and

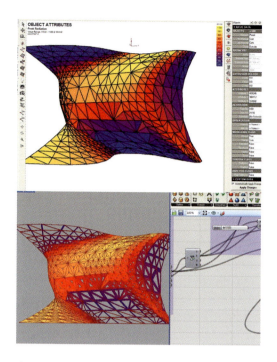

data as the essential design driver, rather than architect's intuition." [4] In nonlinear computation, the performance simulation is no longer simply a way to evaluate the final form, but is the engine of form generation. Performance-based design method can be used to "measure actual quantifiable data, as well as analyze and predict behavior of the system." [5] For instance, when the PBD method is used to design a building facade with curtain walls, the curtain wall panels can be customized according to the solar radiation map of the building façade. A parametric model can be built with a sequence of deformation and control nodes tothe building façade. Then morphing controls can be added to the prescription and yield a matrix of morphed curtain wall panels that act independently according to local solar radiation data. With the connection between data input and corresponding geometric variations across the façade, designers can create a high degree of complexity and consequently explore the dynamic possibilities of tiling with performance analysis. [6]

INTRODUCTION

1.4 USING AUTODESK MAYA FOR PARAMETRIC DESIGN

3-D modeling technology has been extensively developed in the past two decades. Today, architects are using various algorithms, scripts, and simulated physics to generate complex forms that move beyond the traditional digital drafting and modeling operations. There are many parametric design software programs including Maya, Rhino, Generative Component, CATIA, and others.

1.4.1 Case studies

Autodesk Mayahas been widely used in the film and game design industry to create animations and special effects.[7] Due to its comprehensive tool set and great potential for parametric design, more and more architectural and interior design firms, such as Greg Lynn Form, Zaha Hadid Architects, and Gage/Clemenceau Architects, are adapting Maya and integrating it into their design work flow.

5900 Wilshire, Greg Lynn Form. This new anchor on the corner of Wilshire and Ogden makes for a gateway as well as a pedestrian destination and entry into the 5900 Wilshire complex of landscape, plaza, and tower lobby. A branching network of columns supports a 45 foot by 180 foot lattice roof structure that varies in depth from 6 inches to 10 feet; allowing for mottled shading and constant comfortable light levels during the day throughout the year. The roof lattice supports a network of computer-controlled color and intensity changing lights that make for a dynamic but subtle light show, designed by the motion graphics studio Imaginary Forces, on the boulevard after dark. This roof spans across the main entry staircase of the building, framing a gateway to the building from Wilshire Boulevard. The restaurant building is designed in harmony with the columns and is composed of gently tapering, curved drum-shaped volumes that are clad in stainless steel.

INTRODUCTION

H2 House, Greg Lynn Form. The H2 House is a multi-functional visitor and demonstration center for the display of new solar and low energy technology located at the public entry to the OMV Austrian National Oil company in Schwechat, Austria on the outskirts of Vienna. The design of the building utilized state of the art computer simulation software to model the solar performance of the building throughout the year. These simulations were used to generate the actual shape and form of the building along with the alignment and shape of all shading devices and the photovoltaic cells. The north facade of the building was shaped through the simulation of the automobile movement on the highway. The sweeping surfaces reveal the interior of the building in different patterns when viewed from the autobahn both arriving and departing the city.

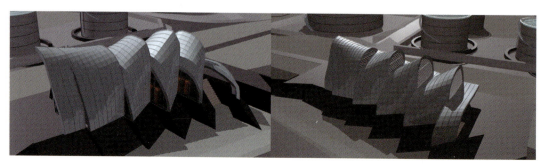

INTRODUCTION

Embryological House, Greg Lynn Form. The Embryological House employs a rigorous system of geometrical limits that liberate an exfoliation of endless variations. This provides a generic sensibility common to any Embryological House at the same time that no two houses are ever identical. This technique engages the need for any globally marketed product to have brand identity and variation within the same graphic and spatial system; allowing both the possibility for novelty and recognition. In addition to design innovation and experimentation, many of the variations in any Embryological House come from an adaptation to contingencies of lifestyle, site, climate, construction methods, materials, spatial effects, functional needs and special aesthetic effects. For the prototyping stage six instances of the Embryological House were developed exhibiting a unique range of domestic, spatial, functional, aesthetic and lifestyle constraints. There is no ideal or original Embryological House as every instance is perfect in its mutations. The formal perfection does not lie in the unspecified, banal and generic primitive but in a combination of the unique intricate variations of each instance and the continuous similarity of its relatives. The variations in specific house designs are sponsored by the subsistence of a generic envelope of potential shape, alignment, adjacency and size between a fixed collection of elements. This marks a shift from a Modernist mechanical kit-of-parts design and construction technique to a more vital, evolving, biological model of embryological design and construction.

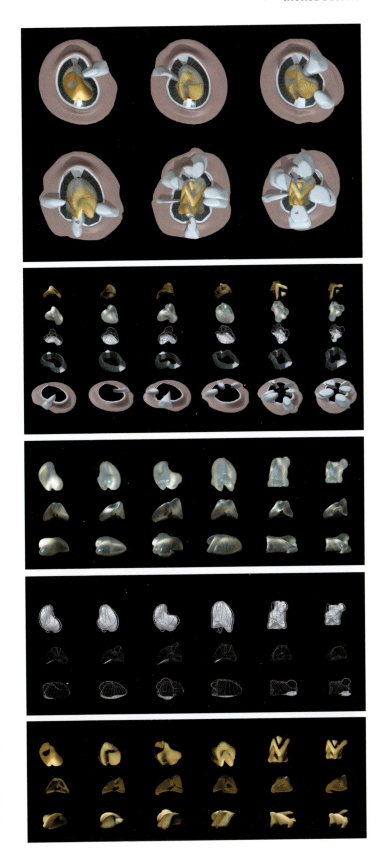

21

INTRODUCTION

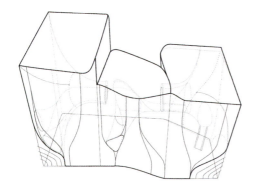

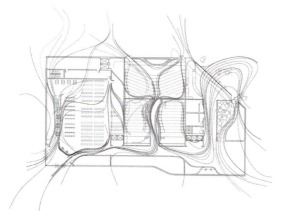

Estonia Academy of the Arts, Gage Clemenceau Architects. In the past decade architectural design has become increasingly reliant on the limited form-making tools offered in standardized architectural software packages. Recent projects from Gage / Clemenceau Architects, such as this competition entry for the Estonian Academy of the Arts, have actively researched the digital tools used in distant design disciplines in an attempt to move beyond normally unchallenged design boundaries within the architectural profession.

The facades, apertures, and large courtyard manifold openings of this project were designed using the software package Alias Studio (similar as Maya surface modeling toolset), which is typically used for automotive design. By creating an experimental alliance with the software manufacturer, Autodesk, the architects misused the software with the express purpose of cross-pollinating automotive and architectural design tactics. Instead of relying on platonic geometries which typically guide architectural design decisions, the facade of the Estonian Academy of the Arts is entirely, and tautly, wrapped in what the automotive industry refers to as "Class-A" surfaces—surfaces which produce the maximum aesthetic effect with a minimum of mathematical description. The building contains both purely aesthetic fluid ripples and contours, as well as performative scoops, tunnels and vents that funnel fresh air to all areas of the building—from the lobby to the interior courtyard, to the 5th floor central manifold featured in the center of the overall composition.

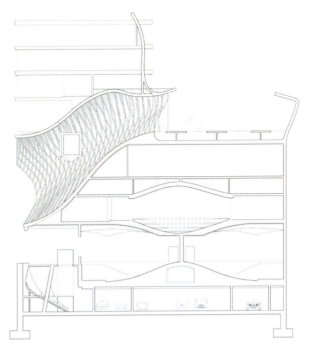

A large-scale prototype panel was constructed of the centralized section of the building in order to view these surface-based geometries at a larger, architectural scale. To be more specific, automotive design is largely based on the placement of "break lines,"— the folds in panels which reach along the side of a car from the front to the back. The portion of the panel above the break line reflects the sky; the portion below it reflects the road. Careful curation of the break lines, therefore, allows car designers to capitalize on the relation between the viewer, the object, the ground and the sky— which is a problem normally specific to architecture, and generally solved through massing.

This problem was addressed more specifically in the prototype panel, which was produced to research how a logic of break lines and reflection might produce a new genre of relationship between the building and its viewer. Instead of break lines running horizontal, as in a car, the break lines run vertically, allowing facade panels to fold and reflect various views of the sky and city around the site depending on one's relative location to the building.

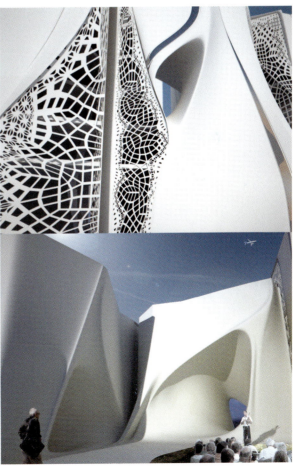

INTRODUCTION

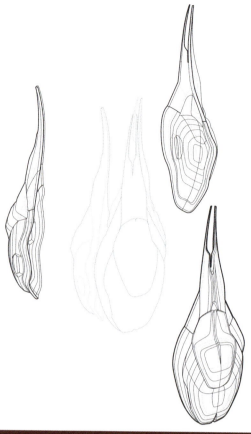

Solar Flower, Gage Clemenceau Architects. Solar Flowers were designed to be woven into the urban fabric of the city. Acting as a fountain or monument, the solar flowers would become a focal point to be enjoyed by the public, while simultaneously harnessing the sun's energy with the use of solar technology. Mechanical components inside the flowers were designed to follow the natural opening and closing patterns of real flowers. Once fully bloomed the flowers would expose interior petals lined with solar panels, technologically mimicking nature by collecting solar energy before automatically closing with nightfall.

INTRODUCTION

INTRODUCTION

Agriculture Network in Milan 2030, Tang & Yang Architects. The architects designed both the large scale vertical structure and the small scale spaces between buildings to demonstrate how social diversity can be ensured in Dergano. These loosely bounded aggregated spaces, characterized by porosity and local interconnectivity, serve as meeting and gathering places. They provide opportunities for play, movement, activity, and the experience of nature for everyone. A polycentric and web-like green loop, a relatively narrow and tree-lined boulevard that comprises bicycle routes and elevated pedestrian paths is developed to connect individual farm blocks. The resulting interlocked pattern is emphasized both horizontally and vertically in the skyscraper. By offering a laminated weave of twin structures (a solid residential tower and a vertical farm with 1:1 ratio), the project explores various combinations of artificial spaces and natural spaces to create a cohesive and interactive landscape.

INTRODUCTION

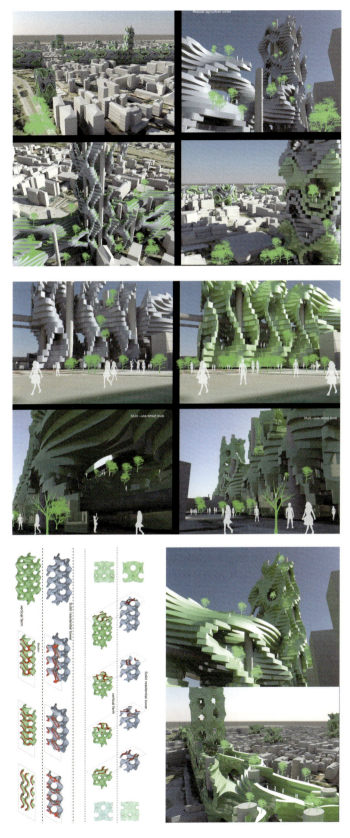

27

INTRODUCTION

Interview with Fulvio Wirz, Zaha Hadid Architects

Fulvio Wirz is the lead Architect at Zaha Hadid Architects (ZHA). He has worked on a number of award winning projects both as an architect and designer including the Eli and Edythe Broad Art Museum, Michigan and the KAPSARC in Saudi Arabia. He has also been the project designer on Aura and the Zephyr Sofa which have been featured in exhibitions such as "Zaha Hadid and Suprematism" in Zurich and "Andrea Palladio and Contemporary Architects" in Venice.

Ming Tang: Please tell us about your role at Zaha Hadid Architects.

Fulvio Wirz: I joined ZHA in December 2005. Since then I have been working on more than 30 different projects, mainly as project architect. Despite being responsible for my team coordination I like to stay fully involved in every design aspect of the project. This includes concept generation for which my software of choice is Maya.

Ming Tang: How do you collaborate with other designers in the team?

Fulvio Wirz: The way we structure our team and workflow does really vary depending on scale and design stage of the project we are working on. What is shared by all our teams here at ZHA is a unique and creative approach to design in which each member can give his contribution to the final result.

For instance when we start a new project for a building we always invest a few weeks for concept generation. At this initial stage all the designers are asked to propose a draft concept for the building. The goal is to work on multiple spatial configurations using several form finding

strategies to explore all possible ideas. Once the final concept has been chosen we divide the design team according to programmatic areas of the building which might be individually developed within the boundaries traces during the initial speculative phase. A coherent generative approach allows us to make changes to our scheme while preserving the strength of our initial idea.

Ming Tang: Would you please describe the typical workflow of a project at Zaha Hadid Architects?

Fulvio Wirz: At ZHA we use a broad variety of software and this means that team collaboration must be based on a cross-platform process. In order to accomplish that we make extensive use of parts referencing combined with a well structured file naming system. This allows us to keep track of the geometries which have been exported from one platform to another at each stage making sure that each designer, while working on its part, is always aware of the progress made by the others. Maya has superb reference tools and at this stage our 3-D master model is often assembled in that platform.

Ming Tang: How does your team use Maya program in various design stages?

Fulvio Wirz: Maya is a very powerful package. The number of tools and its flexible architecture allow us to implement it at different stages of the design.

Obviously, due to its free-form nature, Maya is widely used at concept stage design for competitions and for product design in which teams can take advantage of its intuitive modeling tools, the wide choice of engines for simulating physical

INTRODUCTION

Aura. Zaha Hadid Architects. (Photograph by Luke Hayes)

behaviours and the infinite possibilities of customization offered through MEL, its internal scripting language.

At this stage we have used Maya to accomplish a broad variety of creative and generative tasks from computing minimal pathways in master-planning to form finding in shell structures, from simulating people flow with fluid dynamics to pure sculpting for product design. The range of opportunities offered by this platform is so wide that I reckon we have barely used 25% of its capabilities in architecture.

Despite this our ZH-CODE research team has been working hard to develop a number of proprietary Maya C++ plug-ins to add project-based custom tools. These custom add-ons allow us to extend the range of utilization of Maya from pure conceptualization to geometrical rationalization and optimization for construction. This usually happens at early stages of the design but gives the opportunity to maximize the efficiency of the concept before exporting the entire 3-D model to a BIM platform for structural and mechanical coordination.

Ming Tang: Since you joined Zaha Hadid Architects, you've worked on a number of projects using various digital design processes. Would you please give us a few examples?

Fulvio Wirz: Since I joined ZHA in 2005 I have been working on a large number of projects at different scales, always trying to experiment and innovate as much as possible and mainly using Maya as the main platform for my researches and projects. One particularly successful design which has been developed in Maya is "Aura": an installation we made in 2009 for a collateral event of the Venice Biennale which was set within the beautiful scenario of a Palladian villa: "la Malcontenta". Our conceptual idea was to translate the linear proportional system used by Palladio into a non-linear chaotic system in which beauty emerges from a complex order. We have then translated the linear proportions in frequencies using sine waves to describe them. The symmetry and simplicity of the resulting shape has been distorted by using non-linear deformers in Maya. The process allowed us to generate several variations, or phenotypes, of the same design by altering the parameters of the deformers and their configurations.

From 2009 to 2011 I have been part of a team of 5 project architects responsible for the King Abdullah Petroleum Studies and Research Center (KAPSARC): a state-of-the art research facility and iconic landmark reflecting the Kingdom's involvement in energy and the environment to be built entirely on a new site located between downtown Riyadh and the King Khalid International Airport. The project sported a cellular aggregative concept in which each element was parametrically reconfigured to adapt to the environmental conditions defined by winds and solar gain. The resulting composition features both local differentiation and overall coherence of language thus it perfectly embodies the idea of parametric field.

Another project which deserves a mention for its innovative use of Maya is the Liquid Glacial Table, a transparent dining table which uses refractive properties of water to accentuate its curved legs while keeping the top perfectly flat and usable. For this project we have used Maya n-particles to simulate the complexity and behaviours of water flow with all its waves and ripples. Emitters have been placed to describe the layout we envisaged for the legs and water has been digitally poured from them against a flat surface defining the table top.

Ming Tang: Are there any unexpected challenges during the design?

Fulvio Wirz: When your aim is to innovate you can always expect to face challenges but you can rarely predict them. Zaha used to say that without this feeling of uncertainty there is no real progress. This said a mature and coordinated design

INTRODUCTION

1551_King Abdullah Petroleum Studies and Research Centre. Zaha Hadid Architects. The design approach for the King Abdullah Petroleum Studies and Research Center has solid technical and environmental considerations at its heart, but the architecture endeavours to move beyond the individual constraints to create a living, organic form that transcends the simple technical strategies and has a strong expression in and of itself. The research center is by its nature a forward-looking institution, and the architecture also looks to the future with a formal language that can continually expand or transform without compromising the visual character of the complex. A cellular structure of crystalline forms emerges from the desert landscape, shifting and evolving to best respond to environmental conditions and internal functional constraints. Consistent organizational, spatial, and structural strategies drive all elements of the plan. The approach is adaptive. Each unit is differentiated in size and organization to best suit its use. Individual buildings are divided into their component functions, and the forms can readily respond to changes in requirements or arrangements. The architecture is protective from the outside and porous on the inside. While giving a strong, hard shell to the outside, the architecture opens up within as a series of sheltered courtyards that bring softly controlled daylight down into all of the spaces. A system of layering and buffered zones creates soft transitions from the hot and glaring exterior to cool and filtered interiors.

INTRODUCTION

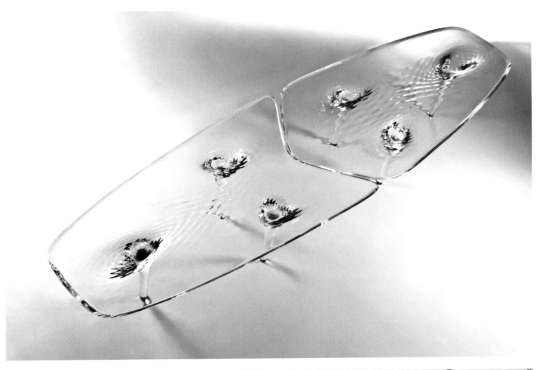

The Liquid Glacial. Zaha Hadid Architects. The Liquid Glacial design embeds surface complexity and refraction within a powerful fluid dynamic. The elementary geometry of the flat table top appears transformed from static to fluid by the subtle waves and ripples evident below the surface, while the table's legs seem to pour from the horizontal in an intense vortex of water frozen in time. The transparent acrylic material amplifies this perception; adding depth and complexity through a flawless display of infinite kaleidoscopic refractions. The result generates a wonderful surface dynamic that inherits a myriad of colours from its context and continually adapts with the observer's changing viewpoint. The form is of its creator; a design that does not compromise functionality or ergonomic requirements and a coherent evolution of her architectural narrative exploring movement through space. (Photograph by Jocopo Spilimbergo)

INTRODUCTION

process and a good team of professionals is able to detect major pitfalls taking the right compromises between risk and innovation. But it goes by itself that a non-standard design means more trials and coordination to perfect the result. As a main innovator in this field, ZHA has grown a reputable experience in complex buildings design.

Ming Tang: Comparing with other free form modeling programs, what do you think are the strengths of Maya?

Fulvio Wirz: As I used to say to my students the major advantage in terms of creativity which Maya has over other similar packages is the fact it was never designed for architecture. This statement might sound like a paradox but it is utterly true in that in Maya also the choice of a tool becomes an act of creativity in its own. In fact some of the best designs we have ever made rely on the intelligence and creativeness of their designer in reinterpreting commands which were intended for a completely different scope. Who could imagine we would end up generating architecture using tools designed to control character's facial expressions (blend-shape) or define minimal pathways using hair simulation or generate masterplans using fluid dynamic!

Apart from that I think Maya has one of the quickest, most intuitive and customizable interfaces ever. The amount of features can be scary and makes for a steep learning curve but in terms of modeling there is a lot you can do with just a handful of commands. Moreover with release 2014 there is going to be a huge step forward in terms of modeling workflow.

Ming Tang: To the designers in the building design industry who are interested in learning Maya as a design tool, what advice would you like to offer?

Fulvio Wirz: So far I don't have a lot of advice to give to my students or to people who wanted to learn Maya for architecture. You can read or watch thousands of tutorials on the web but they will not fully teach you the correct workflow to use the software for design purposes. The reason for that, as I said earlier, is because Maya's architectural workflow has been developed by students and advanced designers all over the world through a creative reinterpretation of its standard commands.

But now I have finally an answer for these enthusiasts who want to step into this unique design experience: just read this book!!

Ming Tang: What do you think of the impact of parametric design in the field of architecture?

Fulvio Wirz: I think in the last decade parametric or generative design has had an impact not only on architectural design but on the entire building and design industry. There is a multiplicity of aspects which have been affected by this paradigmatic shift, as Peter Eisenman likes to describe it, and the entire industry will keep changing, evolving and improving with it. The one aspect, which is already tangible, is the global architectural language. It is undeniable that the repertoire of contemporary architecture has changed following the new scenarios opened by digital software. But I think we are now facing a phase in which the speculative research and the design processes defined in the last decade will eventually reach their complete maturation. The outcome cannot be anymore a new language or a different form finding approach. Parametric design must grow to encompass a broader range of issues and foster a better collaborative environment for multiple disciplines while targeting a seamless integration with manufacturing pipelines.

INTRODUCTION

1.4.2 Nonlinear modeling in Maya

"One way to think about a scene in Maya is that it is a web of nodes. Each node consists of specific information and actions associated with that information."[8] Maya records the history INPUTS nodes in the modeling process. This nonlinear procedural can be realized in Maya by the process of configuring a network of nodes developed by each action. The relations of these nodes are generated through the design procedural based on the constraints applied when geometric forms are constructed. The parametric model is developed by combining INPUTS nodes into a larger system that preserves its relation and hierarchy. For example, when lofting three curves into a surface, Maya will record the curves as INPUTS nodes for the surface and allow modifications of curves when needed. This nonlinear process uses a set of networked nodes to drive the modeling sequence, which surpasses the traditional linear approach.

In Maya, object operation history is saved through a series of sequential operation nodes that form a network. The relations among connected nodes can be viewed by Maya's dependency graph.[9] The object history includes all the input and output nodes that are connected. An object's input nodes are evaluated before the object node itself is evaluated. In the example of lofting three curves into a surface, the surface node relies on one input node named *loftsurface*, which in turn relies on three inputs, curve A, curve B, and curve C. After the loft operation is complete, Maya allows designers to revise the three input curves, update attributes of the loftsurface node such as degree attributes and section span attributes, or even delete one of the input curves. Once the connected nodes are revised, Maya will re-evaluate all the nodes associated within the network and regenerate the model in a split-second manner, which appears as simultaneous update in the display window. This powerful real-time undo–redo process makes nonlinear design more manageable and therefore a popular design approach in architectural design.

By implementing the nonlinear approach in Maya, designers can provide a parametric system that is highly adaptive for future modifications. Many design issues can be solved by capitalizing on the dynamic interaction between parameters and geometric forms. With this engaging experience, architects can explore novel 3-D forms with various modeling, simulation, rendering, and animation

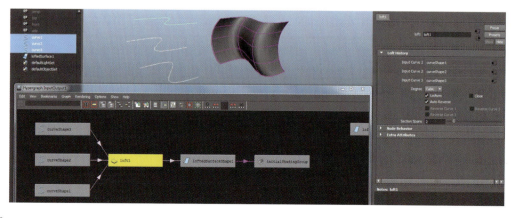

36

tools. The ability to generate, animate, and analyze geometries in Maya often sparks new ideas. Designers can quickly experiment on a large quantity of forms and subsequently optimize solutions. The use of various procedural modeling tools in Maya, including the expression and relation-driven modeling controlled through Maya script, allows parameters to interact with one another. Exploring the parametric computing and fabrication techniques with the emphasis on the potential of fabricating forms has expanded the horizon of architectural novelty and originality into an uncharted territory.

1.4.3 Performance based design in Maya

The performance-based design extends an architectural form into a synthetic information model, which exists for a meaning beyond aesthetic values. With Maya physics engine, real-world physics can be simulated for form-finding. Generative form-finding frequently takes inspiration from the analog world. The form-finding techniques used in projects such as Gaudi's catenary and Frei Otto's wool thread pattern can be either simulated independently or in combination.[10] During simulation, some material properties, such as stretch resistance and rigidity, are introduced into the form-finding process. Maya dynamic simulation provides instantaneous geometric form output responding to predefined forces. These forces range from gravity and wind to collisions among objects, all of which can be viewed as external parameters that transform the initial geometry into a performance-driven form.

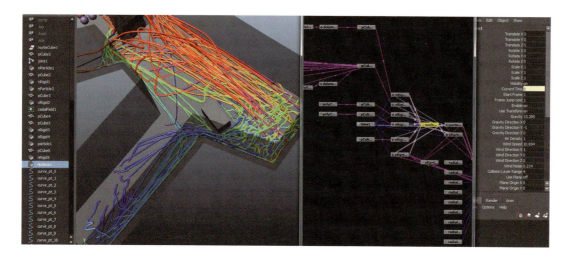

1.5 OBJECTIVE OF THE BOOK

Architecture has become an interdisciplinary collaboration. This book intends to provide architects with an introduction to how to use parametric methods to generate innovative design solutions, with a particular interest in the tools provided by Maya. However, the book is not written as a comprehensive Maya menu book, but focuses on specific procedures that have been proven useful and promising for architecture and interior design. The book will:

- Demonstrate parametric modeling process through Maya NURBS and polygon modeling

- Demonstrate how various parameters can be integrated into a series of design equations and generate solutions through a nonlinear process

- Demonstrate architectural visualization with Maya material, lighting, and rendering tools

- Describe how fabrication techniques such as CNC tool path, laser cut, and 3-D print data file can be generated in Maya

- Introduce performance-based design through Maya physics simulation

- Introduce Maya MEL scripts to generate user interface and execute operations

- Introduce how to integrate Maya with other design programs

1.6 TUTORIALS

1.6.1 Tutorial: Basic Maya interface

1. Create several polygon primitives such as box, sphere, or cube. [11] Maya tools can be accessed either from the menus or the buttons in the tool shelf.

2. Change the display mode from **Wireframe** (hotkey **4**) to **Shading** (hotkey **5**).

3. Hold **Alt + left mouse button** to rotate the camera view,[12] **Alt + middle mouse button** to pan the view, and **Alt + right mouse button** to zoom the view.

4. Use hotkey **A** to zoom out the view to display all objects.

5. Use hotkey **F** to zoom view to fit the selected objects.

6. Select an object, hold right click and choose **Face, Edge,** or **Vertex** in the pop-up menu to select certain components from the object, or **Select** in the pop-up menu to choose the entire object. Use **F8** to switch the selection between the object mode and the component mode.

7. Select the entire object. Use **Move** (hotkey **W**), **Rotate** (hotkey **E**), **Scale** (hotkey **R**), or **Select** (hotkey **Q**) to modify the object. Pay attention to the **Attribute Channels** on the right screen and see how the numbers are changed when modifying the object.

8. Select several components such as vertices, faces, or edges, and use **Move, Rotate,** and **Scale** to modify them.

9. Turn on the grid display and **Snap to Grid** button in the tool bar. Use **Reference Window** to control the unit and grid dimensions. When creating a new cube, its corner points will be locked to the grid.

10. Use **Space Bar** to switch the viewport from four views to a single view.

11. Use **Outliner** from the **Window** menu to observe all objects in the scene. Hold **Shift** key and select several objects and group them with hotkey **G**, or **Group** tool from the **Edit** menu. If moving the group node, all children objects within are changed accordingly. **Ungroup** the objects from the **Edit** menu if needed.

1.6.1 Step 6

INTRODUCTION

1.6.2 Tutorial: Nonlinear modeling with Maya

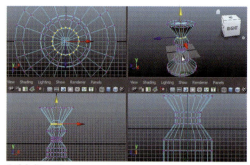

1.6.2 Step 3

1.6.2 Step 4

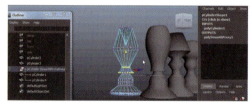

1.6.2 Step 5

1. Create a cylinder and define its **Transformation Attributes**.

2. Select the cylinder. Click its **INPUTS** node on the right side of screen, and modify the **polycylinder1** parameters such as **Subdivision** and **Radius**.

3. Manipulate the object on the **Vertex** level and make it like a lamp. Choose **X, Y, Z** axis handlers to control the manipulation during the operation.

4. **Duplicate** the lamp (hotkey **Ctrl + D**) and **Smooth** it.[13] Now in the **INPUTS** node, the **Smooth** action is recorded as **polySmoothFace1,** and all parameters related to it are accessible. Change the **Division** value from 1 to 2 and observe the difference.

5. Click the **Smooth Proxy** button to create a connection between the low polygon model and its smoothed high polygon version. Move the smoothed object away from the original one. Manipulate the original object on the component level, and observe how the smoothed version is updated in real time.

6. Apply **Boolean** operations,[14] such as **Union, Difference,** or **Intersection,** on the object level to two objects. Pay attention to the pivot point after the Boolean operation, which can be moved back to its geometric center by **Center Pivot** tool.[15]

7. Apply **Bevel** operation on the selected edge.[16]

40

INTRODUCTION

1.6.3 Tutorial: 2-D pattern making in Maya

This exercise explores how to generate a complex pattern by using a simple polygon plane. The complexity is built up by a sequence of selections and operations on both vertex and face levels. The pattern made in Maya can be easily exported as 2-D files for laser cutting or exported as 3-D models to other program for further manipulation. It is an efficient way to design complex architectural systems, such as curtain walls and space frame, starting from a simple pattern concept.

1. Create a polygon plane. In the **INPUTS** node, define the subdivision **Width** and **Height** as 20.

2. Right click the plane and hold the right mouse button. Select **Vertex** component in the pop-up menu, then select a point in the plane.

1.6.3 Step 2

3. Double click the **Selection** tool on the left screen. Check **Soft Selection** option from the pop-up **Tool Settings** panel, and define the **Falloff Radius** value by using the slider. Now multiple vertices are highlighted with gradient colors.

4. Adjust the **Falloff Radius** value to increase the soft selection range.

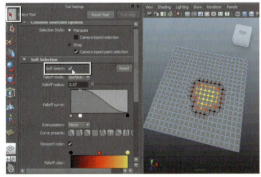

1.6.3 Step 4

5. Use **Scale** (hotkey **E**) to scale the selected vertices. Notice that the transformation has a gradient smoothing effect across the selected vertices. Now the rectangular grid pattern is transformed into an organic pattern, which is still quad based. Each face is formed by four edges.

6. Select the entire object and use the **Chamfer** tool, which breaks each vertex into multiple points and pushes

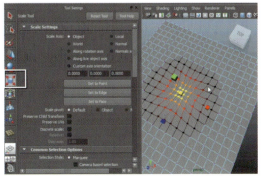

1.6.3 Step 5

41

INTRODUCTION

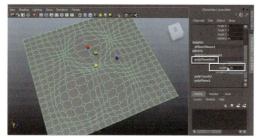
1.6.3 Step 7

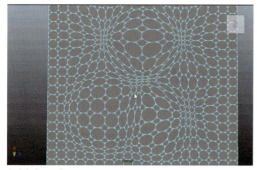
1.6.3 Step 8

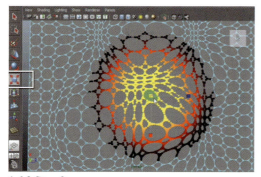
1.6.3 Step 9

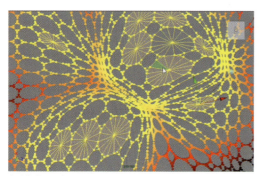
1.6.3 Step 9

them along the connected edges. The result is similar to cutting off each corner with specific dimensions.

7. Under the history **INPUTS** node, there are two files named *polychamfer* and *width*, which allow designers to input a value between 0 and 0.5. If the value is set as 0.5, each new generated point will be pushed against the neighboring vertex along the edge. As the result, the grid will be transformed into a diagonal pattern. The **Width** value is typically defined as 0.25 or 0.3, resulting in a honeycomb pattern.

8. The **Chamfer** tool can be repeated several times to achieve smoother corners, which will transform the honeycomb pattern into a circular pattern. This operation increases the number of polygon faces significantly.

9. Use **Soft Selection** and **Scale** tools to deform certain areas to create an organic effect.

10. Use the **Poke Face** tool to break a face based on its centroid. For example, a triangular face can be broken into three triangular faces, while a quad (four edges face) can be broken into four triangular faces. When **Poke Face** is applied to multi-edge faces, a radical pattern is formed based on the new vertex generated in the centroid of each face.

11. Use the **Extrude** tool to extrude faces to create an offset or ring effect. By dragging the scale manipulator, the new faces can be scaled interactively. The scale value can also be defined accurately by typing the values in the **Transformation Attributes Channel**.

12. Select large faces by holding the **Shift** key and select them one by one. Then

Extrude the selected faces together.

Tip: Make sure the **Keep Face Together** option is off under the **Edit Mesh** menu so each face can be transformed independently.

13. **Scale** down the extruded faces. Define the **Division** value in the history **INPUTS** panel to create more subdivisions along the extrusion.

14. Use **Delete** key in the keyboard to remove the new generated faces to create holes in the plane.

Tip: The **Extrude** tool can also be used to extrude vertices. When selecting and extruding multiple vertices, a complex pattern can be created by adding divisions and manipulating the **Width** value. Set the **Length** value to 0 to keep the face flat, otherwise many extruded pyramids will be generated.

1.6.3 Step 13

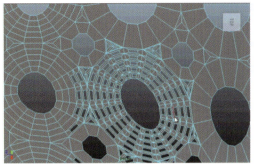

1.6.3 Step 14

1.6.4 Tutorial: Polygon frames

This tutorial demonstrates how to use polygon modeling to create a frame structure, which can be customized with various thickness or subdivisions. Two methods are introduced in this tutorial. Both methods use the Extrude tool to generate new faces and then delete some faces to create openings. However, they use different settings in the Extrude operation. Method A is based on the Offset value from the original edges, while method B is based on the Scale value to shrink the original faces.

In method B, the new faces are generated by scaling the original faces based on their centroids. Therefore the thickness of the frames is not uniform in this method, while method A creates the same thickness because the same offset value is used to

INTRODUCTION

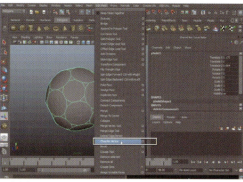

1.6.4 Step 2

1.6.4 Step 4

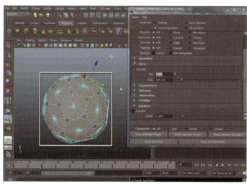

1.6.4 Step 5

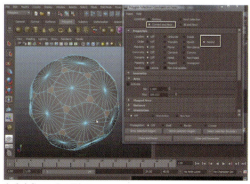

1.6.4 Step 5 (Tip)

generate the frames.

1. Create a simple polygon **Soccer** ball.

2. Use the **Chamfer** tool to add complexity on each face.

3. Choose the **Select Using Constraints** tool from **Select** menu in the **Polygons** menu group. Right click and hold the mouse button and choose **Face** component as the select type.

4. Activate the **Next Selection** option in the **Polygon Selection Constrains on Face** window. Check the **Area** option in the **Geometry** tag. Adjust the **Area** range between the minimum and maximum values to select all the large faces across the entire object surface.

5. Use **Poke Face** to split the selected large faces based on their centroids.

   Tip: In the **Polygon Selection Constrains on Face** window, **N Sided** under the **Property** tag and **Order** options can also be used to select all the nontriangular and nonquadfaces. Designers can apply further tessellation to these N Sided faces.

Method A

6. Make sure that the **Keep Faces Together** option is off.

7. Open the **Extrude Face** tool box. Set **offset** value to 0.01, and then click the **Apply** button. The offset value may need to be adjusted several times to achieve the desired result. When the **Extrude Face** operation is complete, all the newly generated faces are automatically selected by Maya.

8. Use the **Delete** key in the keyboard

to remove these new faces. Now a frame-like soccer ball is created. All the edges are equally offset from their original positions, regardless the size of the faces.

Method B

7. In the **Extrude Face** options window, choose **Reset** in the **Edit** menu to reset all setting to default.

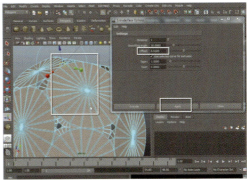

1.6.4 Method A, Step 7

8. Set **Offset** value to 0 (by default) and click the **Apply** button. All the new faces are automatically selected after the Extrude action. The position manipulator is shown as arrow heads and scale manipulator as small boxes. Three handles are provided along **X, Y, Z** axes. Drag one of the small boxes in the scale manipulator to scale the new faces along one direction.

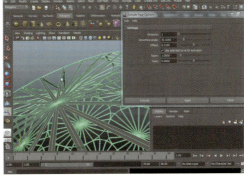

1.6.4 Method A, Step 8

9. Drag another small box from the scale manipulator to scale along another direction.

10. The scale value, set between 0 and 1, can also be manually defined in the **Extrude** node under the **INPUTS** node.

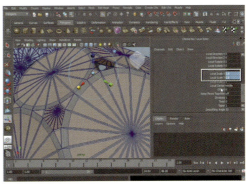

1.6.4 Method B, Step 10

11. Delete the news faces by using the **Delete** key in the keyboard. Notice that the thickness of the frames is not even in this method.

1.6.4 Method B, Step 11

45

MAYA MODELING

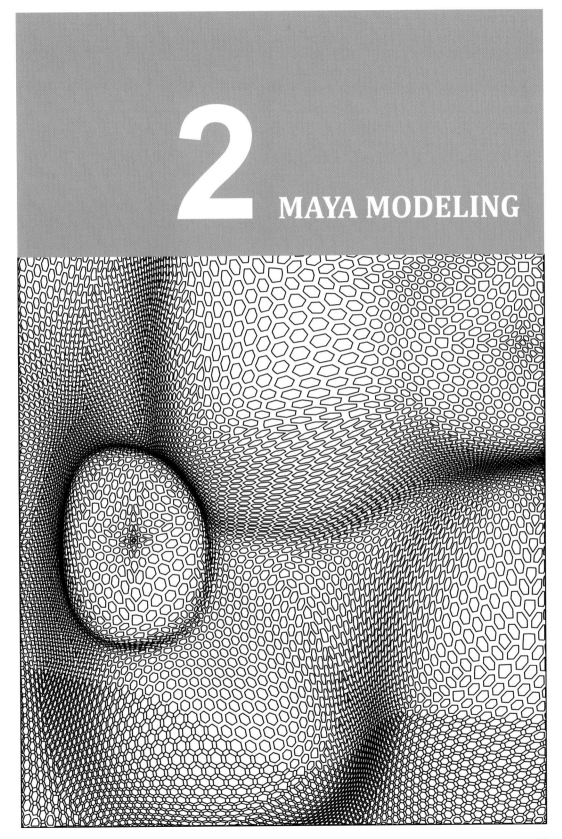

2 MAYA MODELING

The modeling process is one in which a series of 3-D objects is generated. Three modeling techniques exist in Maya: polygonal modeling, NURBS modeling, and subdivision modeling. Because subdivision modeling is an extension of polygon modeling with smooth and coarse control, this chapter discusses only the polygonal modeling and NURBS modeling.

2.1 POLYGON MODELING

A polygon model is a group of polygon faces that includes essential modeling components such as vertices, edges, and faces. The edge component can be constructed based on two vertices. On the other hand, a triangle, the simplest face, can be created by connecting three vertices. More complex polygons can be made by using a series of triangular faces. The vertices, edges, and faces formulate the hierarchy of a polygon model. A group of polygons connected by shared vertices is called a *mesh*.

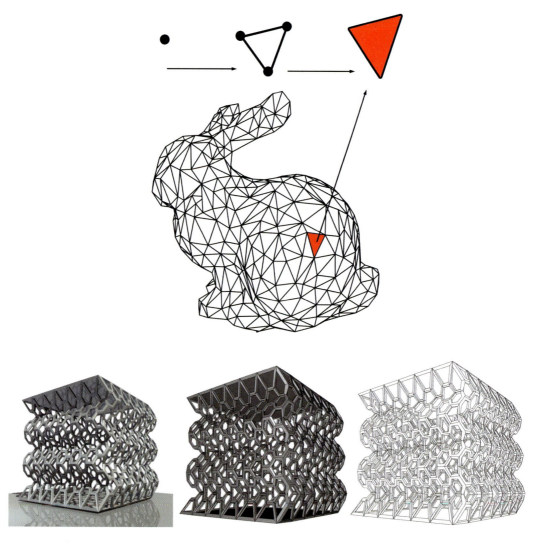

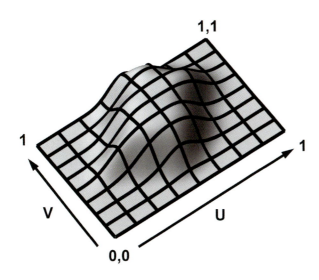

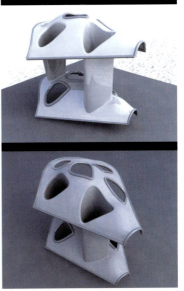

2.2 NURBS MODELING

NURBS (Non-uniform rational B-spline) is constructed by intersecting curves that are driven by mathematical formula. A NURBS surface can be created by operations such as revolving or lofting curves. A NURBS surface has U and V coordinates to define the direction of curves, along with U and V values to define the subdivisions of controlling vertices (CVs) along that direction. UV values can also be used to position a control vertex within a surface. For example, the UV value of 0, 0 defines a vertex located at one corner of a surface, while the UV value of 1, 1 defines a vertex at the opposite corner. A NURBS model can be easily manipulated by moving its control vertices.

2.3 CHOOSING THE RIGHT MODELING TECHNIQUE

Generally, polygon modeling is best for creating hard-edge objects, while NURBS is best for smooth and organic objects. In architectural modeling, polygon modeling and NURBS modeling have different strengths and limitations. Polygon modeling is a fast way to create faceted objects. Compared with NURBS, a polygon model can be interacted and rendered faster in real time.[1] Beyond that, polygon modeling provides powerful tessellation tools, which allow designers to panelize a polygon model with complex patterns. Among various 3-D programs, Maya has a wider range of polygon editing tools on both object and component levels, such as Poke Face, Split Face, Cut Face, and Deformer tools. Some polygon tools can even mimic certain NURBS operations with mesh smooth and soft manipulation. Designers can easily smooth a polygon model by subdividing the existing faces. Another advantage of polygon modeling is its direct connection to Maya nCloth simulation engine, which can animate soft objects and apply forces to them. At last, polygon modeling allows designers to control UV texture mapping and bake lighting and material into vertex color. These techniques are essential for real-time rendering and game-engine driven visualization.

Parallel with its strengths, there are limitations of polygon modeling as a composed mesh of faces. Above all, it lacks the accuracy of NURBS and prohibits designers from creating a precise model, such as the surface of a vehicle. It is also difficult to convert a polygon model into a NURBS model. Last, a polygon model could be "messy" if it contains illegal components such as overlapping faces and zero area faces.[2]

NURBS is the best choice if designers want to create an amorphous, organic object. A NURBS surface can be constructed based on several curves. Because Maya records all actions in the history INPUTS node, designers can access these historical values and manipulate the original curves in a nonlinear fashion. A NURBS model can be easily trimmed with intersection objects or projected curves as well. Simple surface patches can be joined together to create complex objects. These operations are easier to use than polygon Boolean operations.[3] The level of detail of a NURBS model can be controlled by rebuilding the UV values, which is more effective than the Reduce or Add Divisions tools in polygon modeling. Furthermore, a NURBS model can also be easily converted into a polygon model to take advantage of all polygon-editing tools.

One of the limitations of a NURBS model is its complexity and slower speed of interacting in real time. NURBS surfaces need to be converted and welded into a single seamless polygon model to be animated with Maya animation tools, which can handle polygon models much faster than it handles NURBS models. It is also difficult to add or modify finished details in a NURBS model compared with a polygon model where the Split Face, Edge Loop, and Extrude tools in polygon modeling are much more powerful in controlling details on either vertex, edge, or face levels. Meanwhile, NURBS modeling is difficult to use when creating a faceted object. For instance, a NURBS cube is made of six individual planes and is more difficult to manipulate than a simple polygon cube is.

MAYA MODELING

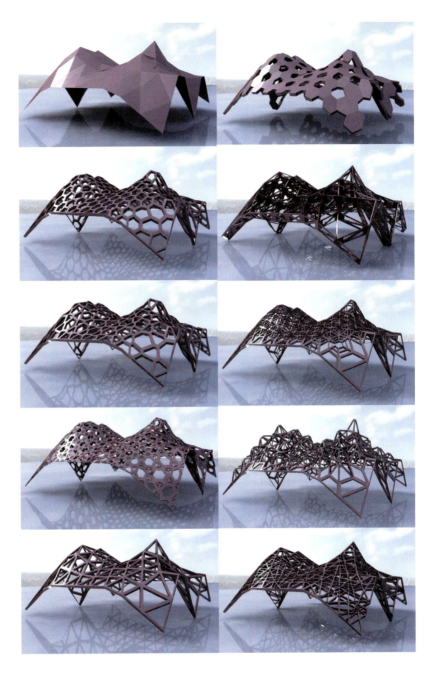

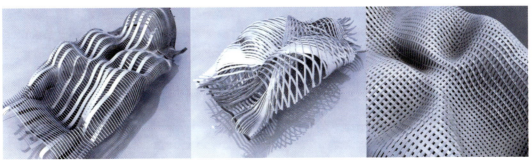

2.4 CONVERSION BETWEEN POLYGON MODEL AND NURBS MODEL

In Maya, a NURBS model can be converted into a polygon model or a subdivision model. Designers can choose various methods to tessellate the NURBS surface to a polygon model. For example, the standard fit method uses the curvature of the NURBS surface to control the size of individual polygon faces and represent the NURBS surface with an adaptive tessellation. The results could be a heterogeneous tessellation, depending on the complexity and topology of the NURBS model. Maya maintains the relationship between the NURBS model and the polygon model unless designers delete the INPUTS history.[4] By manipulating the CV points of the original NURBS model, designers can observe the converted polygon model automatically updating in real time. Designers can also convert a single NURBS model into multiple polygon models with different tessellation methods and settings. As soon as the origin NURBS model is reconfigured, all the polygon models will update simultaneously. The Super Extrude MEL script [5] can also be added to generate a complex frame-like structure, which inherits all the NURBS tessellated patterns.

Can designers convert a Maya polygon model back to NURBS model? The answer is yes and no. Unlike Rhino,[6] Maya does not provide a direct conversion from polygon meshes to NURBS surfaces. However, designers can convert a polygon model into a subdivision model that could then be converted into a NURBS model.[7] An alternative way is to extract the polygon edges to a series of curves and loft these curves into a NURBS model.[8]

2.5 TUTORIALS

2.5.1 Tutorial: Tessellation and iterative building skin

1. Create a simple NURBS surface by lofting several curves.

2. **Rebuild** the surface by setting UV values of 10 and 10. Make sure the surface degree is set to 3 Cubic.

3. Convert the NURBS surface into a polygon model. In the **Options** window, set **Type** to Quads, **Tessellation method** to Count, and **Count** value to 100. Click **Apply**.

4. Move the newly generated polygon model away from the original NURBS surface. Name it *polygon01*.

5. Set the **Count** to 1,000 and convert the same NURBS surface to another polygon model. Move it away from the original NURBS surface. Name it *polygon02*. Use the same method to create three more polygons and name them *polygon03, polygon04, polygon05*.

6. Right click and hold on top of the original NURBS model, select **Control Vertex** (**CV**) and manipulate certain CV points to deform it. Now all the converted polygon models will update simultaneously.

7. Select *polygon01*. Choose **Poke Face** to break apart the face based on centroid. Repeat several times to create a complex pattern.

8. Choose the *polygon02* and apply the **Chamfer** action. Similarly, **Chamfer** can be applied several times to increase the complexity. The designer can also apply the

2.5.1 Step 3

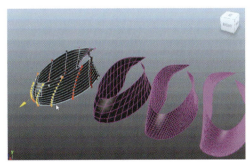

2.5.1 Step 5

2.5.1 Step 8

MAYA MODELING

Poke Face action after the **Chamfer** action.

9. Download the **Super Extrude** MEL script online. Copy texts and paste them into the **Script Editor** window.

10. Select the script and use middle mouse button to drag it to the **Shelf**.

11. Click the **MEL Script** button. The **Super Extrude** window will pop up. Set the **Extrude Scale** to 0.9 and **Extrude Height** to -0.1.

12. Click the **Create Extrude** button. This tool uses every edge to create a frame-like structure.

13. Apply the **Chamfer** action three times to *polygon03*. After getting the circular pattern, select the big circles, and use **Poke Face** to break them into a radial pattern.

14. Apply the **Super Extrude** MEL script and get the frame structures.

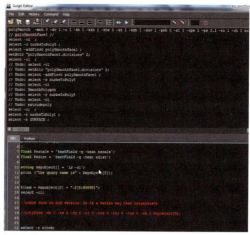

2.5.1 Step 11

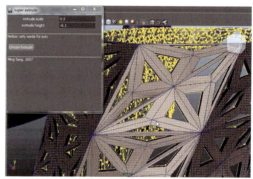

2.5.1 Step 12

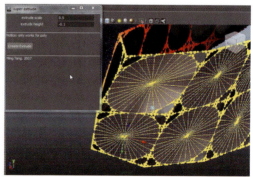

2.5.1 Step 13

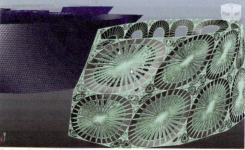

2.5.1 Step 14

MAYA MODELING

15. Apply the **Smooth** tool to subdivide an existing low polygon model.

16. Create another iteration by **Triangulating** *polygon04*. Then use **Chamfer** to create a hexagon pattern.

17. Select a few vertices and **Extrude** them along the normal direction. Set the **Division** value to 10 to create a spider web pattern.

18. Use the **Super Extrude** MEL script to generate a frame structure.

19. Use the **Cut Faces** tool to slice *polygon05* along several random axes.

20. Select several faces and **Extrude** them along the normal direction.

21. **Extrude** the new faces generated in step 20. Scale them to create smaller faces and then delete the smaller faces to create window openings.

22. Apply **Smooth** with **Division** value set to 2.

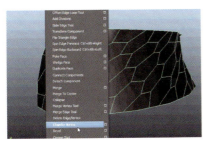
2.5.1 Step 16

2.5.1 Step 17

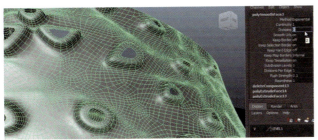
2.5.1 Step 19

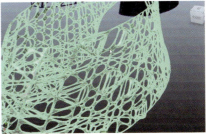
2.5.1 Step 22

2.5.2 Tutorial: Parametric beam and roof

1. Create a simple NURBS plane. Modify several CV points to deform it into an amorphous surface.

2. **Rebuild** the NURBS surface with higher UV values. Set **number of spans U** and **number of spans V** to 20.

3. Use **Soft Selection** to select a group of CV points. Define the **Falloff radius** to manipulate the selection range. Then move the selected points along Y axis.

4. Use **Convert the NURBS to Polygons**, set **Count** to 200.

5. Select the newly generated polygon, use the **Center Pivot** tool in the **Modify** menu to set its pivot point to the geometric centroid.

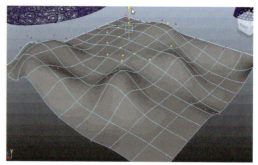

2.5.2 Step 1

2.5.2 Step 2

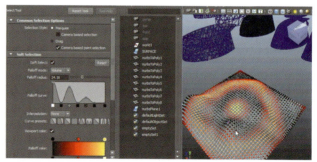

2.5.2 Step 3

2.5.2 Step 4

MAYA MODELING

6. Right click and hold on top of the polygon model and choose **Edge** as the selection component.

7. Drag the selection window to select all the edges.

8. Use **Extrude** in the **Edit Mesh** menu to extrude all the edges. The Manipulator will appear in the view.

9. A blue color circle should show up which allows the designers to switch the local coordination (based on faces' normal direction) to the global coordination (based on the World XYZ axis).

10. Drag the arrow head along Y axis of the manipulator to extrude all the edges.

11. **Convert** the edge selection to the face selection.

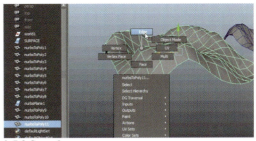
2.5.2 Step 6

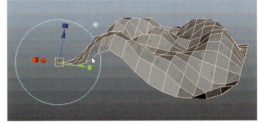
2.5.2 Step 8

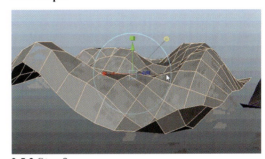
2.5.2 Step 9

2.5.2 Step 10

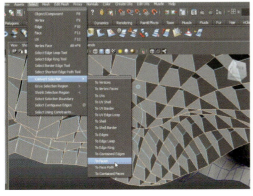
2.5.2 Step 11

57

12. Now all rib faces should be selected. Use the **Triangulate** tool in the **Mesh** menu to divide each face into two triangles.

13. Another option of Step 12 is to use the **Poke Face** tool to divide each face into four triangles.

14. Apply the **Super Extrude** MEL script to generate all the frames.

15. The original roof surface can also be overlapped to create the roof surface.

2.5.2 Step 12

2.5.2 Step 13

2.5.2 Step 14

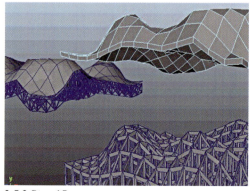

2.5.2 Step 15

2.5.3 Tutorial: Deformation (NURBS + polygon)

Maya Deformer tools can be used to modify a finished model to create iterations during the design process. This tutorial demonstrates how to use NURBS surface as a deformer to modify a complex polygon model. This technique can be used to manipulate a complex wall system or a building skin with a relatively simpler reference surface.

1. Open the example file named *bio_wrap.ma*. The file contains a complex polygon model which has already been applied a Ramp shader.

2. Create a simple NURBS plane under the polygon model. Make sure its size roughly matches the polygon model. Rename it *driversurface*.

3. In the history **makeNurbPlane1** node, change the **Patches U**, **Patches V** to 10, 10 to add more subdivisions on the surface.

4. Use **Control + D** to make a duplication of the NURBS surface as a backup. Move it away. Rename it *blendsurface*.

5. Select the polygon model. Hold **Shift** key to add the NURBS surface named *driversurface* into the selection. Click the **Wrap Deformation** tool in the **Deformation** tool bar. The same tool is also accessible from the **Create Deformers** menu under the **Animation** menu group.

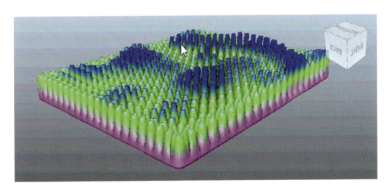

2.5.3 Step 1

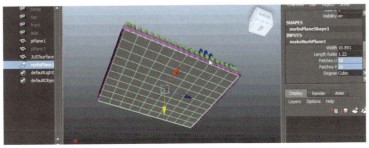

2.5.3 Step 3

6. Now the polygon model is deformed by the NURBS surface. Certain CV points can be selected on *driversurface* to manipulate the surface. The polygon model should automatically update based on the driver NURBS surface.

7. *Driversurface* can also be flattened by selecting all the CV points, highlighting their Y values in the **Channel Box,** and typing 0 to reset them.

8. Use **Blend Shape** to create a relationship between two NURBS surfaces so one surface can be used to control the other. This method is useful when the designers need to control the magnitude of the deformation in certain circumstances.

9. Select the NURBS surface named *blendsurface*. Manipulate its CV points to transform it into an organic form.

10. Select *blendsurface* again. Hold **Shift** key to add the NURBS surface *dirversurface* into the selection. Click **Blend Shape** to connect them. Now *blendsurface* will drive *driversurface.* In another word, *driversurface* will blend into *blendsurface*.

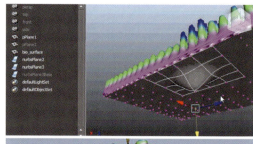

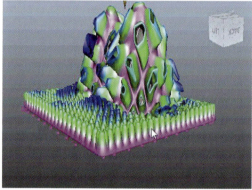

2.5.3 Step 6

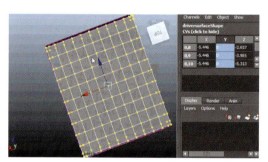

2.5.3 Step 7

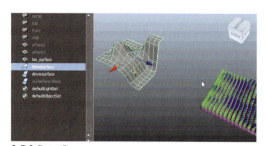

2.5.3 Step 9

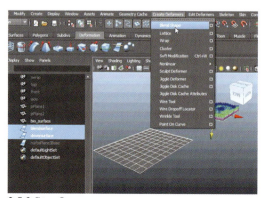

2.5.3 Step 8

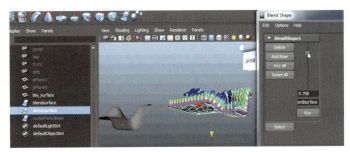

2.5.3 Step 11

11. Go to **Animation Editors** under the **Windows** menu and click **Blend Shape**. Open the **Blend Shape** control panel, which allows the designer to use a slider to define the magnitude value between 0 and 1. Drag the slider to observe how *driversurface* is morphed into *blendsurface*, and how the polygon model is deformed in sequence.

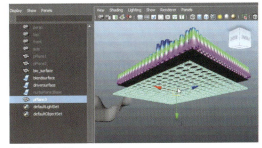

2.5.3 Step 13

12. Continue to modify *blendsurface* to observe the results.

13. Create a new polygon model and attach it to the existing *driversurface*. First, create a frame system by **Chamfer**, and **Super Extrude** a polygon plane. Name the model *base_frame*.

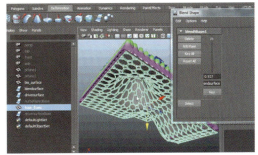

2.5.3 Step 15

14. Select *base_frame*. Hold **Shift** to add *driversurface* into the selection. Click **Wrap** to create a new wrap deformation.

15. Drag the slider in **Blend Shape** window. Now both *base_frame* and the original polygon model will deform gradually together as one single system. Both polygon models are controlled by the wrap deformer *driversurface*. The *driversurface* is controlled by the *blendsurface*.

61

MAYA MODELING

3 PARAMETRIC RELATIONSHIP

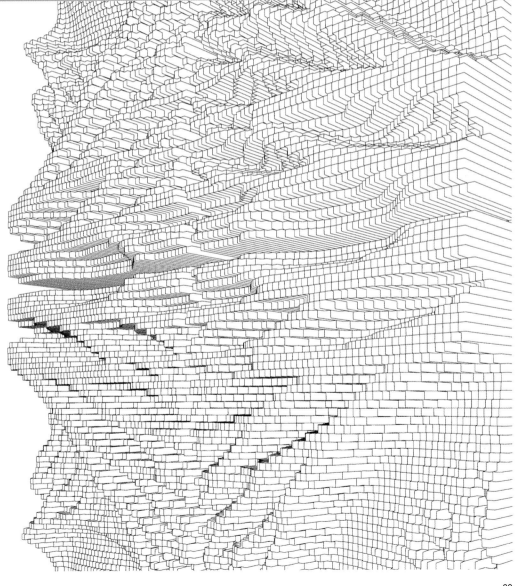

3.1 MORPHING AND BLENDING

Maya provides various innovative modeling techniques that can be adopted in architectural design to produce parametric forms, such as Blend, Skeleton System, nHair, nCloth, and Particle System. Morphing, called *blending* in Maya, is one of these tools.

Morphing is the concept of changing an image from one to another, or manipulating the 3-D geometric transition between two static models. 2-D images can be blended by mathematically combining the transparency values and red/green/blue (RGB) values from multiple images on the pixel level. The color values of each image, usually between 1 and 256, can be multiplied by the layer opacity value in Photoshop, which provides various layer-blend options and graphic outputs. Similar to blending 2-D images with layers, the 3-D morphing technique also uses a mathematic definition of the transition weight. The 3-D morphing technique is widely used in motion pictures to create special effects such as transforming a character from one appearance into another. Maya offers a great tool set to record the morphing process and manipulate the smooth transition. It also enables designers to key frame a morphing animation based on multiple blend targets, which can later be baked into a sequence of iterations and a permutation of all possible transitional status. For example, two pitched roofs with different slopes can be blended together to generate all the sloped roofs in between.

From the computational perspective, the morphing process is not operated on the object level. It is computed on component-vertex level by morphing one vertex into another vertex. Basic knowledge of point parameters is essential to understand this morphing process. In Maya, a point, or vertex, is primarily identified by its identity number (point ID) and spatial position, among which, spatial position is recorded either by an X, Y, Z Cartesian coordination system or a U, V, W spatial

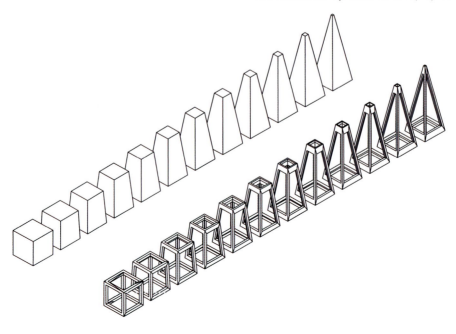

reference system.[1] A point contains a point ID as well as other properties such as vertex color or other user-added values. In addition, Maya can add a series of properties assigned to a particular point, including vertex color, mass and weight, dynamic constraints, and others. In morphing operation, a point ID is used to find a pair of points, each from one object. The first point's X, Y, Z values are gradually changed to the second point's X, Y, Z values. This process can be visualized by creating a trajectory between two points and moving the first point to the target point along the path. By projecting the first point to a different target point, designers can change the morph target.

The Maya Blend tool provides a graphic interface with a weight slider to control the morphing process, which is one of its unique advantages compared to other morphing processes. The weight value has a range between 0 and 1. When the weight value is set to 0, no morphing occurs and the original object maintains its own shape. When the weight value is set to 0.5, the original object will morph half way to the target object. When the weight value is set to the maximum value 1, the original object will completely morph into the target object. This smooth transformation process generates an interim geometry for each substep and presents the complete morphing operation with a series of sequential geometries to generate an animation pass. Therefore, such animation can be frozen at any substep so that the geometry generated for that particular substep can be baked and extracted as an independent geometry that can be treated as design iteration or becomes the base of other modeling or rendering operations. This morphing process is particularly powerful when combined with the PBD concept to optimize iterations based on the

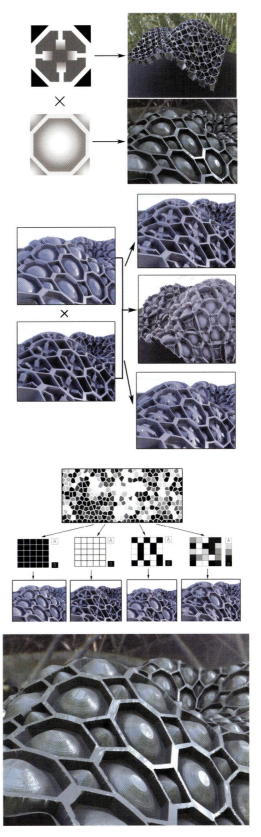

PARAMETRIC RELATIONSHIP

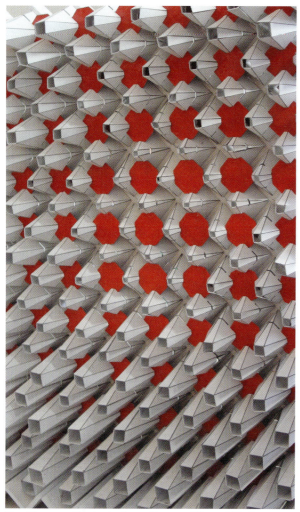

By Theresa Bort, Andrea Suever, Mary Wischmeyer, Rebecca Doughty.

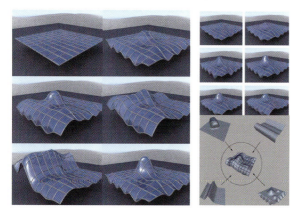

predefined criteria. For instance, designers can use the solar radiation data to drive the morphing process of the paneling system on a building façade to optimize the sunlight control.

From the computational perspective, building models can be mixed with morphing techniques in Maya. Genetic evolution theory can describe the logic of blending different building types. Based on genetic evolution theory, the building form can be understood as a phenotype, which is driven by its genotype (parametric code or DNA). In the breeding process, the genes are mixed and passed from both parents to the offspring. As the result, the offspring carries characteristics from both parents as a hybrid entity. Similarly, the new building form could be the hybrid of two existing building types and carry the values from both. Maya blending is a design methodology, and it should not be considered the same as genetic algorithms such as cellular automation and L system.

For instance, to find a unique roof form that can present ideal values from multiple existing roof types, designers can blend various roof forms, such as domes, flat roofs, or gable roofs, to seek a new roof design solution. The genotype is the transformation values of each point on the roof surface, and the phenotype is the overall roof topology. Maya Blend can animate a smooth transition across all roof forms and generate various in-between roofs. These hybrid results carry characteristics such as drainage, load distribution, or aesthetic values, which can be further evaluated by the designer.

PARAMETRIC RELATIONSHIP

3.2 TUTORIAL: HYBRID HOUSE

1. Use Maya polygon modeling tools to create a simple house model including a basic roof, floor slabs, columns, and walls.

2. **Combine** all geometries into one single object (*building#1*).

3. Duplicate *building#1* twice to create *building#2* and *building#3*.

4. Manipulate the faces, vertices, or edges of *building#2* to create a different building type.

5. Select both *building#1* and *building#2*. Create a blend shape from the **Create Deformers** menu.

6. Open the **Blend Shape** window. Drag the slider and observe the morphing process.

7. Use **Linear Bend Deformer** to deform *building#3* into a different shape.

8. Select *building#3*. Hold **Shift** key to select *building#1* to create a new blend shape.

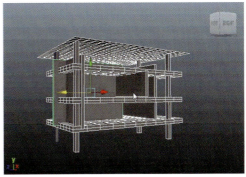

3.2 Step 1

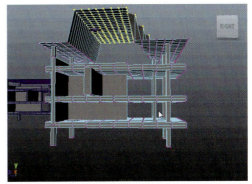

3.2 Step 4

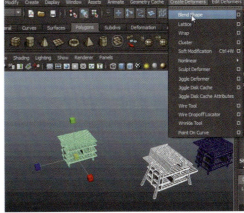

3.2 Step 5

3.2 Step 6

67

9. Now there are two sliders in the **Blend Shape** window allowing *building#1* to morph to a hybrid form from the two target forms (*building#2* and *building#3*).

10. Duplicate *building#1* once again to create *building#4* and use **Separate** to break apart the combined geometry.

11. **Move**, **Scale**, or **Rotate** the separated *building#4* and reconfigure its roof, columns, floor slabs, and walls.

12. Combine the geometries of *building#4* back into a single building by the **Combine** tool.

13. Create a new blend shape relationship between *building#1* and *building#4*. A new slider is created in the **Blend Shape** window.

14. When dragging the new slider, the designer may see *building#4* morphing and flying toward *building#1*. This problem can be fixed by selecting all the vertices of *building#4* and move them closer to *building#1*.

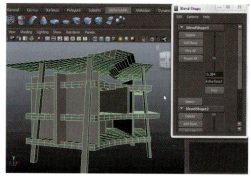

3.2 Step 9

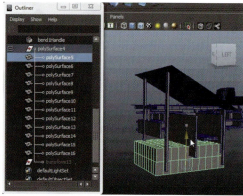

3.2 Step 11

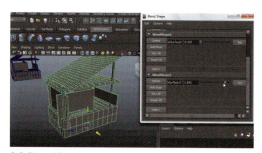

3.2 Step 13

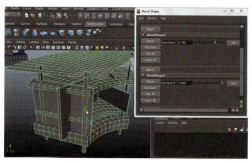

3.2 Step 14

PARAMETRIC RELATIONSHIP

3.3 DRIVEN KEY

Set Driven Key is a Maya animation tool that can be used to set up a parametric relationship between attributes from one or multiple objects. Designers can create a key that links two attributes at certain values. One attribute, serving as the driver, can drive another keyable attribute in the driven object. This driver–driven relationship is originally designed to help in producing animation in the motion picture industry. One application is double-door animation. To animate a double door where both doors swing open, both of the two door panels need to be animated. Designers can link the left door's rotation attribute to the right door's rotation attribute. As the left door is opened, the right door will be opened simultaneously.

In architectural design, the driver and driven attributes can be the X, Y, Z transformation attributes, the object's history INPUTS parameters such as the subdivision values and dimension values, or other numeric values. The driven attribute is updated as soon as the driver attribute is changed.

3.3.1 Driven key controlled morph

Maya Driven Key is powerful to connect certain attributes to the morph weight and create relationships across multiple objects. For example, a typical residential tower can be made by stacking the typical floor plan. However, from the design perspective, residents might prefer a wider view and a larger balcony to enjoy the surrounding landscape when the elevation gets higher, while the lower levels may need smaller windows due to the noise and pollution from the street. Designers can manipulate the typical floor

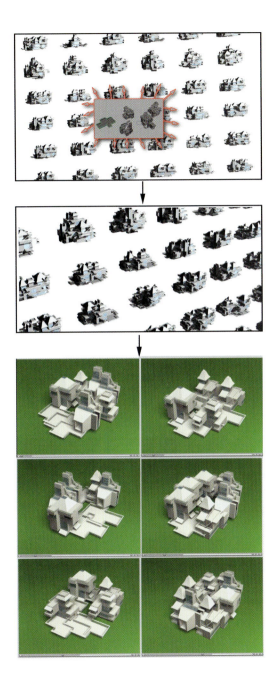

PARAMETRIC RELATIONSHIP

plan to create an alternative plan and blend these two plans with the Maya Blend tool. In a simplified condition, a parametric relationship between two attributes, elevation and the morphing weight, can be generated. After loading the typical floor plan into Maya's Set Driven Key window, designers can define the driver attribute as its Translate Y attribute, which is the floor elevation, while the driven attribute is the morph weight to the alternative plan. The morphing weight is between 0 (0% morph to alternative plan) and 1 (100% morph to alternative plan). This relationship is established by keying a pair of attributes and locking the values. For instance, Translate Y value 0 can be locked to morph weight 0, and Translate Y value 500 can be locked to morph weight value 1. As the result, when the floor plan is raised from the bottom to the top, it will morph gradually from the typical plan to the alternative plan. At the end, designers can freeze all the transitional floors and create the tower.

3.3.2 Attractor controlled morph

Another design application of the Driven Key tool is populating morphing objects over a large surface. Here, different morphing objects are weighted differently to create heterogeneous effects. In this process, the morphing weight is set as a value between 0 and 1. This weight value is parametrically controlled by an *attractor*, a point that drives other parameters and can be selected and moved to test corresponding results. Typically, the distance value between the attractor and the morphing object is used to drive the morphing weight. In this case, the attractor can be described as the center of a magnetic field. The magnitude value decays at a linear rate as the distance value goes up. Designers can use an attractor to

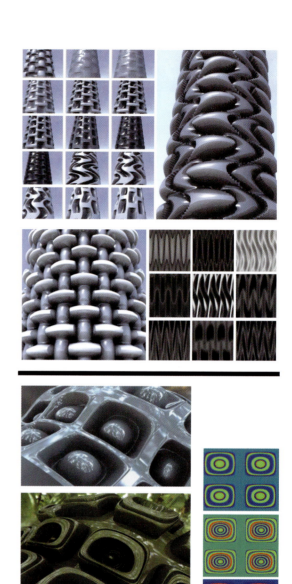

affect the object's morphing weight. The objects located closer to the attractor will morph more than the ones farther away from the attractor.

In architectural design, an attractor can be used to drive the size of an opening on a panel. Each panel is analyzed to calculate the distance value from its centroid to the attractor. Then the distance value is used to control the size of the openings parametrically. The same approach can be applied in large-scale urban models as well, where attractors can be defined based on urban economic nodes, transportation nodes, or highly populated areas, and used to control the buildings' morphing weight according to various topologies, densities, or floor/area ratios (FARs). As the result, designers can visualize the city's development potential.

As a nonvolumetric entity, a locator is a simple point data representing the attractor in Maya program. Locator has standard attribute channels such as X, Y, Z Translate, Rotation, and Scale. Designers can add additional attributes to the locator such as the distance value, which can be linked to other attributes to create a parametric relationship.

3.3.3 Case study: Folded paneling system

A folded paneling system is an example of using attractor, Driven Key, and morph techniques. To create a folded paneling system driven by an attractor, designers can first create a morphing panel by blending two panels. One represents the unfolded status, while the other represents the folded status. These two panels must have an equal number of points, and two points must have a matching ID number to create a pair in the corresponding position. This critical

match usually is achieved by duplicating the original panel to create its identical clone, which has exactly the same number of points and points' IDs. Then the clone can be transformed into a different panel by manipulating its points, edges, and faces. To maintain the connection between the two panels, the number of points should not be changed during the process. Designers can blend these two panels using the Maya Blend tool. The morph weight can be manipulated to control the smooth transition from the original panel to its morphed target. Drag the slider (weight value between 0 and 1) in the Blend window to morph the object in real time.

To simulate panels driven by the lighting conditions, use a Maya locator to represent a point light and calculate the distance value between the locator to each panel. Using the Set Driven Key tool, the distance attributes and morph weight can be locked to create interactions between the light and each panel. The panel will be folded when the light gets closer and will be unfolded when the light is reduced. At the end, designers can simulate this adaptive system with each panel operated based on the light location. Other than the attractor and Driven Key techniques, the morphing weight can also be controlled by the RGB values of a bitmap. This technique will be covered in Chapter 9.

In theory, all quantifiable parameters in the physical world can be integrated into the design equation to formulate parametric relationship. These parameters include, but are not limited to, light, temperature, humidity, orientation, curvature, load, and social and economic data. There are unlimited possibilities for building the parametric relationships between these parameters into a building form.

PARAMETRIC RELATIONSHIP

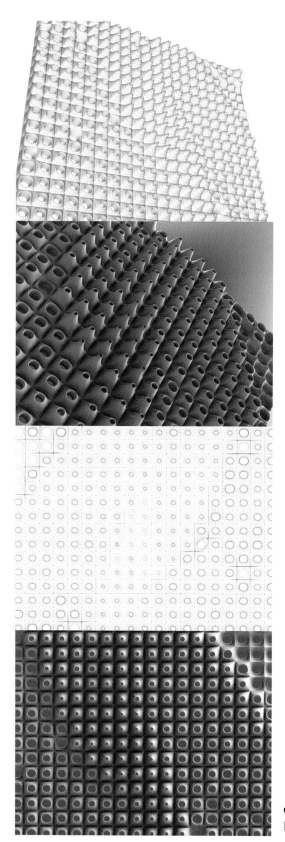

**Case study:
Folded paneling system**

PARAMETRIC RELATIONSHIP

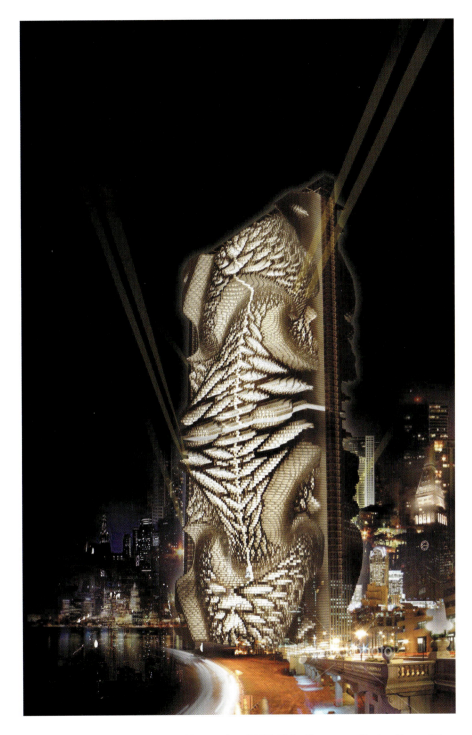

Geno Matrix Skyscraper, Honorable mention, 2007 eVolo Skyscraper Design Competition, Tang & Yang Architects.

This project explores a new prototype of skyscraper which exhibits characteristics of a living organism that evolves in responding to its environment. It is a genotype driven structure that evolves and produces infinite scenarios in its evolution process in responding to the changing spatial requirements and urban demands.

PARAMETRIC RELATIONSHIP

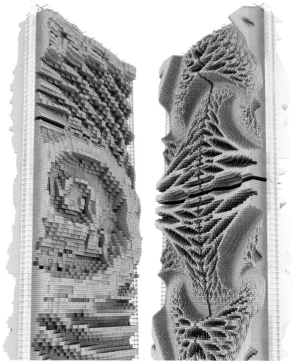

Parent A   Parent B

Rather than using the conventional architectural design process to generate the form, Geno-Matrix comes from genotype, phenotype, mate, crossover, morph, mutation, and selection process. In nature, when two individuals mate, each parent passes half of its paired chromosomes onto its common offspring. The chromosomes combine to form new pairs, which lead to a unique new individual with phenotypes inherited from both parents. Individuals with more adapted genotypes will survive in the evolution process while others will

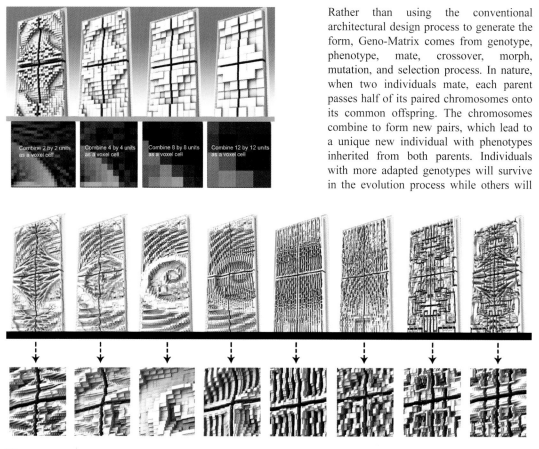

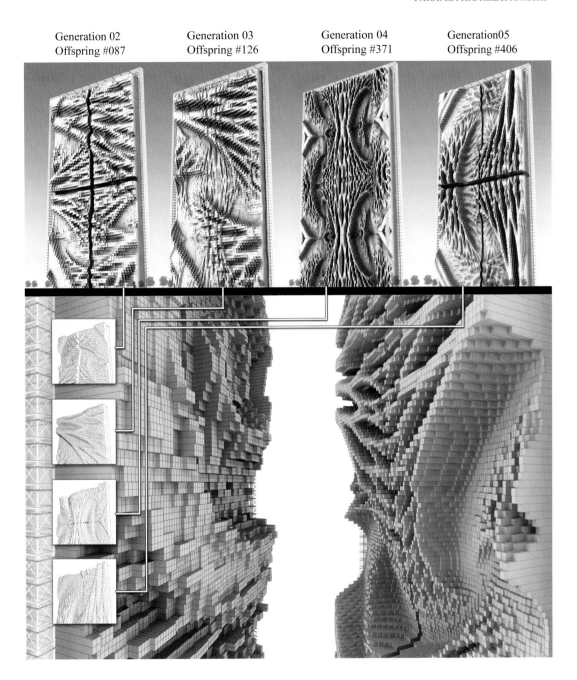

eventually be eliminated. Geno-Matrix can deform itself on the molecular level, being compatible with the unstable fitness of current inhabitation cultures.

In the design process, genetic computing and evolution techniques were applied with the emphasis on their potential of creating meaningful forms in the production of architectural design. The spatial occupancy (SO) model is used to complied sets of contiguous discrete "chunks" of "voxels" to define a solid model. Each voxel (a portmanteau of the words volumetric and pixel) is a volume element, representing a value in 3-D space. A 3-D grid occupied by the object is used to contain all voxels. These volumetric voxels are fixed-size cubes. In the Geno-Matrix model, hundreds of these prefabricated construction units were presented by voxels arrayed in space and thus formulated the presented skyscraper forms. The phenotype was thus represented by the XYZ coordination of each voxel (prefabricated units).

PARAMETRIC RELATIONSHIP

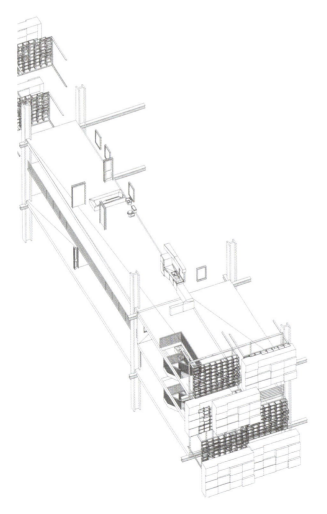

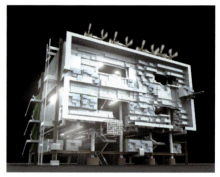

Lego Farm-Reclaim Urban Identity and Food Production, the Third prize, Live the Box competition, AIA Newark / Young Architects Forum, Tang & Yang Architects.

The project utilizes standard height shipping containers as the main building blocks of the structure. By organizing a large quantity of shipping containers on a modular structure system in a manner similar to the Lego game, Lego farm provides mixed-use spaces and integrates sustainable design. This project also explores the solutions of achieving individual consciousness by the use of identical shipping containers from mass production, as a way of reclaiming the urban identity. By modifying each container as a pixel on a large bill-board façade, the project represents a social image of Newark. Similar computer techniques were used as Geno Matrix Skyscraper.

3.3.4 Tutorial: Adaptive skin

1. Create a polygon plane.

2. Use **Poke Face** to split the polygon plane into four triangles. Delete three triangles and only leave one.

3. **Poke Face** twice. Manipulate faces and points to create a basic panel named *panel#1*.

4. Duplicate *panel#1* to create *panel#2*. Change *panel#2* into a folded status.

5. Select both panels and create **Blend Shape** from **Create Deformers** menu.

6. Open **Blend Shape** window and drag the slider to observe the morphing process.

7. Create a locator and move it to the centroid of *panel#1*.

8. Paste the provided MEL script named **Distance Generator** in the tool bar.

9. Select the locator and *panel#1*. Click the **Distance Generator** MEL script to create a new attribute based on the distance between the locator and *panel#1*.

10. Open the **Set Driven Key** window from the **Animate** menu.

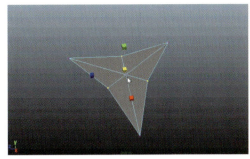

3.3.4 Step 2

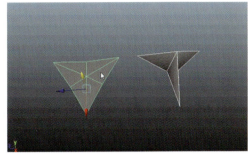

3.3.4 Step 4

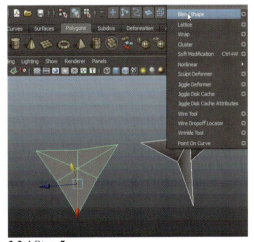

3.3.4 Step 5

3.3.4 Step 9

11. Set the **Driver** as *panel#1's* distance value. Set the **Driven** to the **BlendShape** weight value named **pPlane2**.

12. Move the locator close to *panel#1*. Change the blend shape weight to 0. Click the **Key** button in the window to freeze the first relationship.

13. Move the locator away from *panel#1*. Change the blend shape weight to 1. Click the **Key** button in the window to freeze the second relationship.

14. Now, when moving the locator, *panel#1* will morph according to the distance between the locator and *panel#1*.

15. Open the **Duplicate Special** tool panel. Check **Duplicate input graph**, and **Assign unique name to child nodes** option. Duplicate *panel#1* to create *panel#3*.

16. When opening the **Outliner** window, designers will see that Maya does not only duplicate *panel#1*, but also duplicates the locator and *panel#2* because the locator and *panel#2* are both parts of the history node.

17. Select both locators and move them together. Both *panel#1* and *panel#3* are updated independently from each other in responding to their own locators.

18. Repeat **Duplicate Special** and create an array of panels. Arrange the panels to create a seamless paneling system.

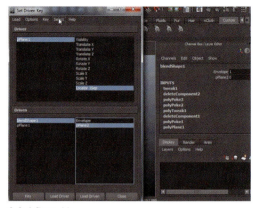

3.3.4 Step 11

3.3.4 Step 13

3.3.4 Step 15

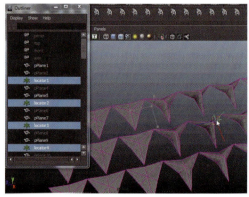

3.3.4 Step 18

PARAMETRIC RELATIONSHIP

19. Use window selection to select locators, and move them together. The entire panel system will be updated according to the locators.

20. Other operations can also be applied on top of the panels, such as **Super Extrude** or **Bend** deformations.

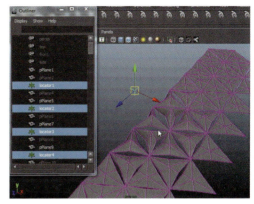

3.3.4 Step 19

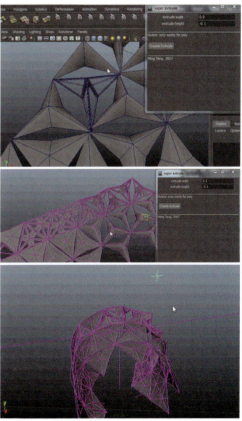

3.3.4 Step 20

79

PARAMETRIC RELATIONSHIP

4 MAYA SKELETON

Maya skeleton is a hierarchical structure composed of a chain of joints and bones that are originally used to animate body movements. Joints are the points of articulation to define the connection of bones as well as the constraints and rules of their rotation. Designers can bind a skeleton to a model, called *skinning*, and thus deform the model. A parent joint is higher in the skeleton's hierarchy and drives the transformations of its child joints.[1] As a special deformer, the skeleton has to be attached or associated to geometries.

4.1 ARCHITECTURAL APPLICATION OF MAYA SKELETON

In architectural design, Maya skeleton can be used to model a kinetic structure that contains moving parts, such as a retractable stadium roof. The most effective way of using Maya skeleton to control an architectural form is the parent-children relationship, which creates a hierarchy among a series of objects. Designers can attach an object as a child to a specific joint. As the parent of the object, the joint controls the object's transformation attributes. If designers rotate the parent joint, the child object, as well as the child joints, will rotate with it. Because the transformation is operated on the object level rather than the component level, the object always maintains its original shape.

Designers can use a kinetic skeleton system to simulate the complex folding process of a design. For instance, when creating a folded roof structure that follows a similar movement to an umbrella structure, the entire structure can be controlled by Maya skeleton set in a radial pattern. The modeling process starts with a series of lines to form a rib system, followed by creating a skeleton system to drive the ribs to open and close. A sequence of points is defined along each rib. Purlins are made by connecting the points across neighboring ribs. Creating a hyperbolic form after all points on the ribs are connected is done next. As the result, Maya skeleton can control the rotation of each rib to drive its unfolding process. Meanwhile, the ribs will also drive the movement of purlins. The final outcome is a folded roof structure, similar to an umbrella, which can be folded and unfolded by a single skeleton in Maya.

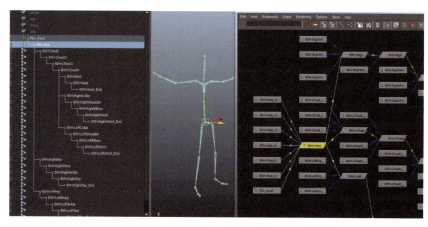

MAYA SKELETON

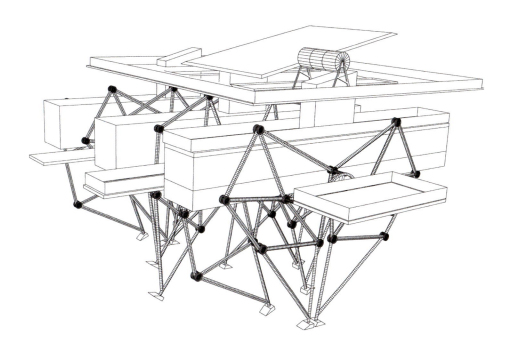

Land Walker-Messenger in Jerusalem, Honorable mention, Just Jerusalem competition, MIT, Tang & Yang Architects.

The central feature of this project is the development of a walking machine named *land walker*, which moves across the land in a manner similar to a mobile house. By giving up the land ownership and walking on the site with rich historic / political background, it carries messages for the city, evolves and forms mutual associations among people, site and event.

MAYA SKELETON

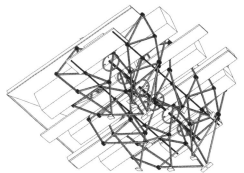

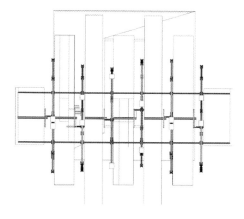

The walking mechanism of *land walker* is inspired by Theo Jansen's walking sculpture. It provides a walking platform as a mobile "site" to host living units. Each living unit is a modular building system that can be prefabricated and assembled on site according to spatial requirements of the user. The entire building is a solar energy driven machine, which can be assembled on the individual unit level, and respond to dynamic changing cultures.

Maya skeleton system was used to create the *land walker*.

MAYA SKELETON

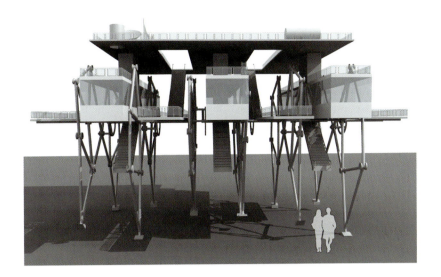

MAYA SKELETON

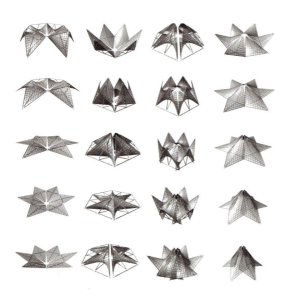

Folded Bamboo House, the First prize, Self-Sufficient Housing competition, Tang & Yang Architects.

This bamboo house is a deformable structure that exhibits characteristics of an umbrella, with the potential of adapting itself to various contexts and functional requirements. It is a self reconstructive structure for easy installation, which, according to the changing internal requirement and external site condition, can produce various prototypes. Rather than using the industry mass production to generate uniform dwellings, the folded bamboo house uses a simple kinetic structure made by bamboo, a bottom-up assembling of complex adaptive system that self-regulates, in opposition to top-down overarching principles.

MAYA SKELETON

All sub-structural members are straight bamboo poles, which are used to create ruled surfaces- helicoids, hyperbolic paraholoid and hyperboloid.

The structure system of the house is prefabricated, transported to a particular site, and customized by its user. The spatial characteristics of a folded bamboo house are determined by the structure's open angle of each rib and the spatial relation among them. With this user customized structure system, the house can react to external stimuli and be transformed within a short time frame.

Maya skeleton system was used for the design.

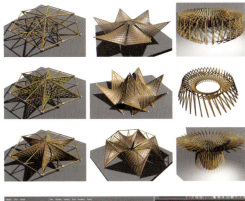

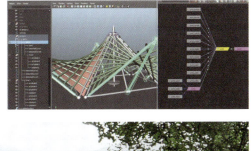

4.2 TUTORIALS

4.2.1 Tutorial: Kinetic radial structure

To simulate a multi-joint radial structure, designers can create an **Inverse kinematics (IK) Handle** to solve the complex chain movement along multiple bones and then duplicate the bones in a radial pattern.

1. In the top view, create a three-joint skeleton. Open the **Outliner** window and check the hierarchy of the joints by name.

2. Create three boxes and make the length of each box the same as the length of each bone.

3. Use the **Outliner** window to watch the list of all objects in Maya scene. Use middle mouse button to drag and drop a box to a joint to associate it as a child to the joint. Repeat this process until all three boxes are embedded within the skeleton hierarchy, each to a specific bone as its parent.

4. Select a joint and rotate it along one axis. The boxes associated with it, and other boxes in the lower hierarchy will rotate with the joint.

5. **Group** the joints and boxes as a group. Use the **Insert** key in the keyboard to activate its pivot point manipulation. Move the pivot point away from the group root. Use the **Insert** key again to turn off pivot manipulation mode.

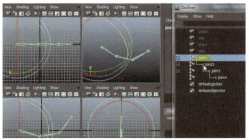

4.2.1 Step 1

4.2.1 Step 2

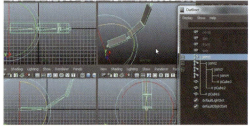

4.2.1 Step 3

4.2.1 Step 5

6. Select the group. Open the **Duplicate Special** tool panel. Set the **Geometry type** to **Instance**, **Rotate** to 10, and **Number of copies** to 36. Click the **Apply** button. Now a radial structure is created.

7. In the **Outliner** window, open the original group node and select a joint. Rotate it along one axis. All other duplicated boxes will automatically follow the rotation since they are the instance of the original group.

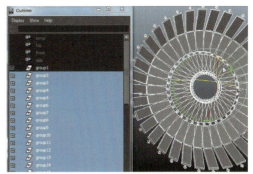

4.2.1 Step 6

The designer can also try an alternative situation, which uses **Smooth Bind** to control a single ribbon like surface rather than three rigid boxes.

1. Create the same three-joint skeleton in the top view.

2. Create a NURBS surface plane and make it match the proportion of the skeleton. Set **Subdivision Width** in the **INPUTS** channel to 50. The goal is to create enough CV points to achieve a smooth deformation.

3. Select the NURBS surface. Hold **Shift** key to add the skeleton into the selection. Choose **Smooth Bind** from the **Skin** > **Bind Skin** menu.

4. Rotate the joints to observe how the surface is bended like a metal sheet.

5. The similar approach can be used to duplicate the surface to create a radial pattern. Repeat step 5 and 7 in the last tutorial.

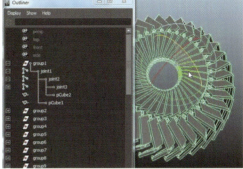

4.2.1 Step 7

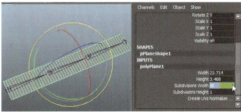

4.2.1 Alternative situation, Step 2

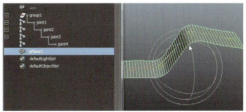

4.2.1 Alternative situation, Step 4

4.2.1 Alternative situation, Step 5

MAYA SKELETON

4.2.2 Tutorial: Walking machine

This tutorial explores how to create a complex Maya skeleton system controlled by the **IK Handle Tool** by constructing a structure similar to Theo Jansen's walking sculpture.[2]

1. Create a simple V shape two-joint skeleton. Use the **IK Handle Tool** in the **Skeleton** menu to connect its start root to the tip of the end. Select the **IK handle** (*IK handle#1*) in the **Outliner** window and move it to observe how the skeleton is driven by *IK handle#1*.

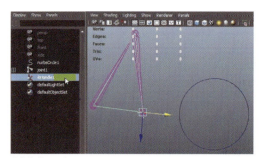

4.2.2 Step 1

2. Create a circle. Move it close to *IK handle#1*. Set the time line to 48 frames.

3. Select both *IK handle#1* and the circle. Use **Attach to Motion Path** from the **Animation > Motion Paths** menu. Now *IK handle#1* is moving along the circle. Consequently, the bone's movement is following the circle as a track.

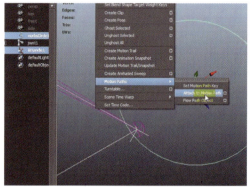

4.2.2 Step 3

4. Repeat the previous steps. Use the **Joint Tool** to create another skeleton controlled by a new IK handle (*IK handle#2)*. Make sure the second skeleton is independent and not attached to the first skeleton.

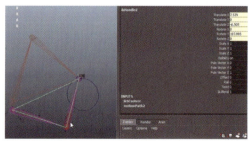

4.2.2 Step 4

5. Select *IK handle#2*. Use the same circle to create a motion path. Now both skeletons are created to form a diamond shape and driven by the circle. Play the animation to test the result. The designer can also move or scale the circle to observe different results.

6. Create the rest parts of the leg that are driven by the existing joints. Start with the same root of the first skeleton. Use the **Joint Tool** to create a three-

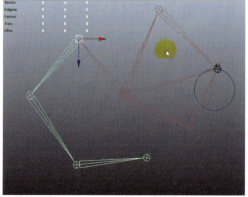

4.2.2 Step 6

90

joint skeleton branch from it. When playing the animation, the designer will see these new parts driven by the existing skeleton.

7. Create a new IK handle (***IK handle#3***) from the second joint (not the root joint) to the tip of the new branches. Test the ***IK handle#3*** and it should only control a portion of the skeleton (two joints) rather than the entire skeleton.

8. Select ***IK handle#3*** and the right joint. Use the **Parent** tool to make it as the child of the existing joint. Now the new branches will follow the movement of other joints too.

9. Use the **EP Curve** tool to create straight lines and complete the rest of the rigid frames. Make the lines the children of the appropriate joints.

10. Model pipes following all the curves.

11. Model gears and other mechanical components.

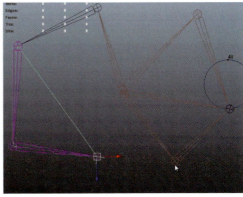

4.2.2 Step 7

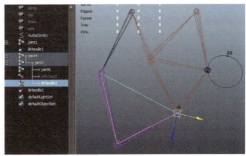

4.2.2 Step 8

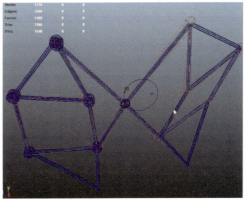

4.2.2 Step 10

MAYA SKELETON

5 SIMULATION

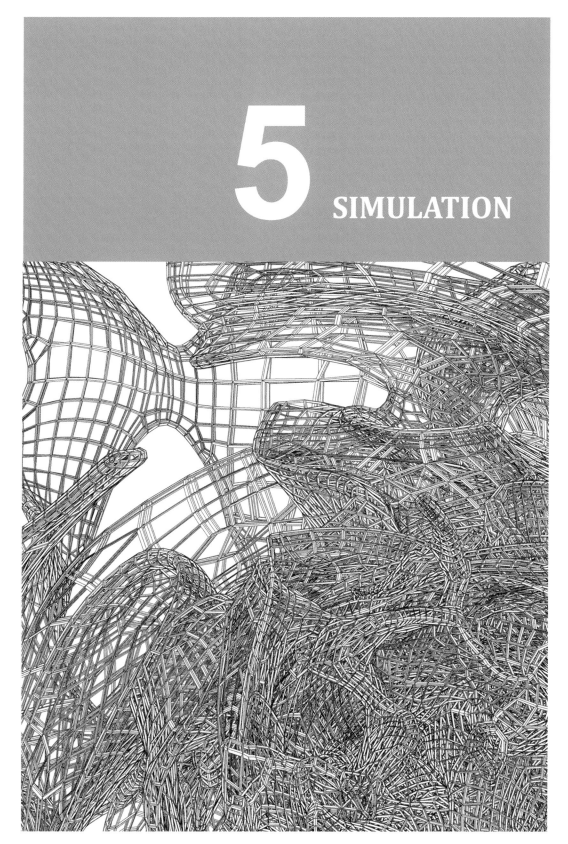

SIMULATION

Computer models can simulate real-world processes to analyze how the systems operate. In architectural design, simulation is a powerful tool to analyze an existing design under specific conditions and generate analytical data to control forms for architectural optimization. For instance, designers can use lighting simulation software to calculate daylight factors and use the result to optimize shading devices, or run a wind simulation by projecting particles onto a skyscraper model to observe the wind turbulence and, therefore, optimize the building mass to minimize its wind load.

Various types of simulation models can be used to gather the performance data of a design model for evaluation. An energy model can be used to simulate thermal and energy performance, a structural model to simulate the load and stress of the structure system, a fluid dynamics model to simulate the drainage of a complex roof system, while a behavior model to create agent-based modeling to simulate path-finding behavior during an emergency evacuation.[1] The results of simulation can be represented by data, diagrams, images, animations, and interactive media.

5.1 SIMULATION FOR PERFORMANCE-BASED DESIGN AND FORM SEEKING

Different from visualization, performance-based design promotes simulation as a design engine rather than an analysis tool.[2] Instead of generating the simulation at the end of the design process, designers can integrate simulation from the beginning and use it to seek ideal forms for the design. This form seeking involves the evaluation and optimization process. It is different from the typical form-making process, which does not include feedback loops. In the form-seeking process, the relationship between the designers and computer is reversed because the computer-controlled simulation becomes the driver and the form becomes the result. After the form is generated, the designer plays the role of the evaluator, and the evaluation criteria can be qualitative or quantitative. The simulation engine will generate an adaptive solution to satisfy the predefined rules. For instance, designers can set the lighting performance goal in Ecotect and let the program find the best form for a shading device to block sunlight from entering a room. Common optimizers are solution-driven algorithms

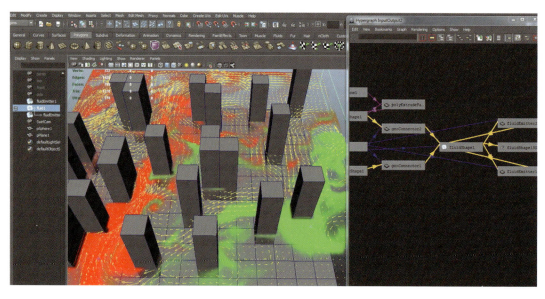

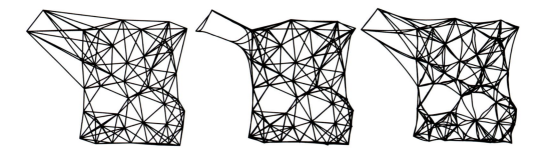

such as the genetic evolution-based solver[3], cellular automation[4], or L-system[5].

5.2 PHYSICS SIMULATION AS AN ARTISTIC DESIGN APPROACH

Physics simulation allows designers to explore forms by setting up a physical relationship between objects and forces. Detached from directly creating and optimizing a single form, designers now have the option to set up rules only for computing and rely on the computer to generate forms. Physics simulation is a form-seeking process. The objective is not optimizing forms according to performance criteria. For instance, after converting a box into an active rigid body, designers can drop the box to a collision plane and capture the trace of its bouncing in Maya. Then the movement of the box can be captured by converting the simulation to key frames. A curve can be added as a child object to the simulated box and it inherits the box's movement. The animated curve is then captured as a sequence of curves, which can be used to create a lofted surface. In this case, the form is not directly manipulated by the designers, but controlled by the properties in the simulation engine such as collision force, gravity, bouncing, and friction. This generative process offers an innovative solution in form seeking based on the simulation of physical properties, which was practiced by Antoni Gaudi and Frei Otto even before the computer era.

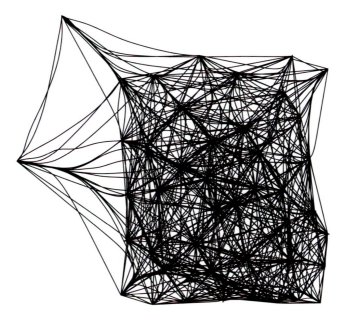

SIMULATION

5.3 MAYA DYNAMICS SIMULATION

Maya dynamics uses rules of physics to simulate natural forces. It includes many systems such as particles, fields, soft and rigid bodies, fluid, and hair. As an extension of classic Maya dynamics, nDynamics is powered by the Maya Nucleus system. Maya nDynamics includes nCloth, nParticles, and nHair systems. These systems can interact with each other through force fields, collisions, and constrains computed by the Nucleus solver.

Similar to Gaudi's form-seeking method with hanging chains, Maya nCloth and nHair systems can be used to create forms driven by external forces. Following the analog method of hanging chain to generate a U-shaped curve, or hyperbolic surface, designers can use selected vertices to create transform constraints in Maya nCloth or nHair. The form will be generated based on gravity and its dynamic properties such as weight, rigidity, and other attributes. The chain will deform and create an anticlastic curve. Designers can use the Maya Nucleus systems like nCloth and nHair to interact with particles, passive collision objects, and various force fields such as vortex and gravity.[6]

Maya nCloth or nHair can be generated by converting regular polygon mesh objects into a network of particles, called *dynamic mesh*. Because the Nucleus solver computes interactions among the particles by creating links between adjacent particles,[7] it is important to control the point network on the mesh

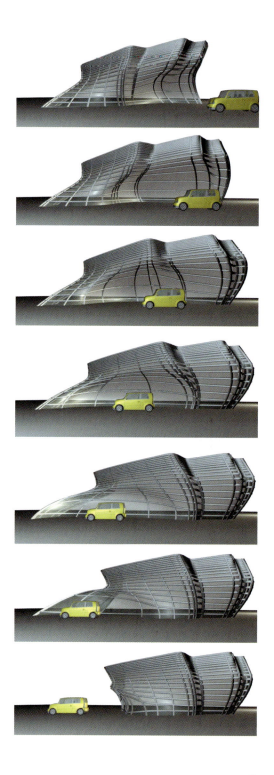

96

surface before converting it to an nCloth. The geometric tessellation will affect the nCloth's simulation behavior, and sometimes can generate "unnatural" results. If a polygon plane is generated with a homogenous grid pattern and then converted into an nCloth, its macro-material properties will be distributed to each vertex in a uniform fashion. If a polygon plane is generated with an irregular tessellation pattern, a series of different geometries or uneven vertex density across the surface, its macro-material properties will be distributed to each vertex unevenly. Forces or constraints applied to these vertices will then trigger different reactions compared to the uniform polygon. This feature is often used to approximate heterogeneous material behavior in the real world. Designers can also remove certain polygon faces within the mesh, trim the polygon, or extrude certain faces before converting to an nCloth. These operations will generate different patterns and result in different simulation behaviors.

Other than the forces set in the force field, nCloth, nHair, nParticle can also interact with other dynamic objects or constraints included in the same Nucleus system. For instance, an nCloth can be dropped on top of collision objects to create the envelope of these volumes.[8] It can also be deformed by an animated locator after linking the constraint points as the children of the locator.

5.4 MAYA PARTICLE SYSTEM AND FORM MAKING

Among the various dynamic systems that Maya provides, nParticles is unique in that it can simulate a large number of points that interact with fields and dynamic objects. Designers can create nParticles and multiple collision objects to generate a path-finding simulation and thus optimize a circulation system according to the found paths. The idea is to establish a meaningful relationship between nParticles and the objects with which they interact. The particles' attributes, such as position, color, and velocity, can be extracted and saved in an exchangeable file format. This file can be streamed into other programs such as Rhino and Grasshopper, in which 3-D forms can be created by capturing the particles' attribute data. Transferring

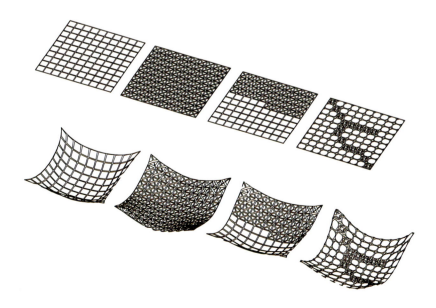

particle data to different software is more complex than transferring static objects. There are universal exchange file formats, such as OBJ, FBX[9], and DXF, which are readable in different software. However, there are no universal standards regarding how to extract particle information.

Besides Maya, Houndi, Realflow, and 3dsMAX also provide various tools, methods, or plug-ins that generate particles and integrate them into the architectural design process.[10]

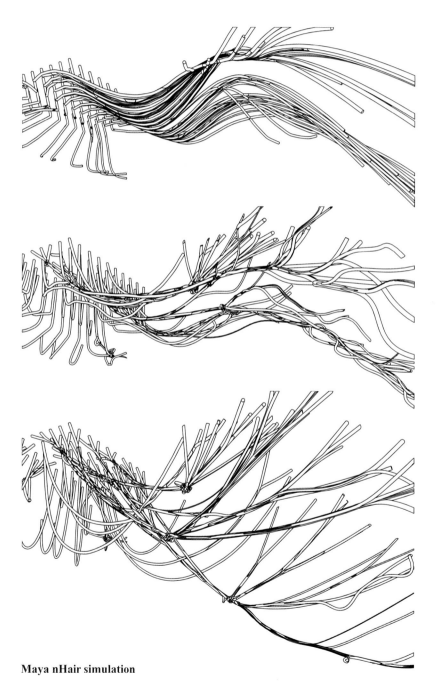

Maya nHair simulation

SIMULATION

Path finding simulation by Maya nParticle.

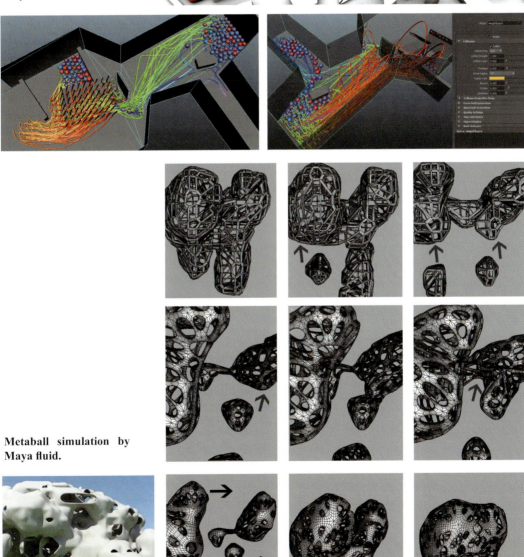

Metaball simulation by Maya fluid.

SIMULATION

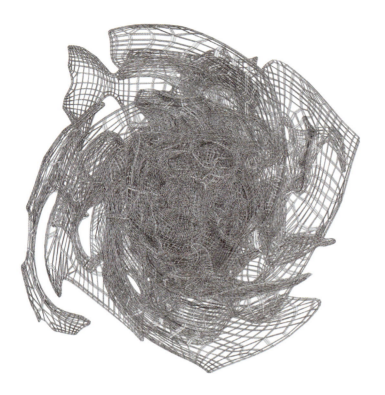

The Tree of Dubai, Tang & Yang Architects.

This project proposes a tower that exhibits characteristics of an ink drop in the water. Rather than using the conventional building envelope, the *Tree of Dubai* uses a 3-D Möbius surface warping around the tower, which provides a continuous network for plant climbing and therefore can gradually transform the building into a green tower.

Maya fluid dynamic was used for this project.

SIMULATION

SIMULATION

Flaming Cube / Taihu Rock, the Second prize, Streetscape in a New World competition, Beijing, Tang & Yang Architects.

The objective of this project is to develop multi-functional urban structures for downtown Beijing that exhibit both modern and traditional Chinese values. The project proposes a serial of organic structures used for a variety of functions. These structures as an entire group have provided an ambiguous meaning on the individual unit level, and created a balance between the old and new. When aligned along the street, the structures' unique forms could stimulate the audience to seek the symbol and message behind them.

Maya fluid dynamic was used for this project.

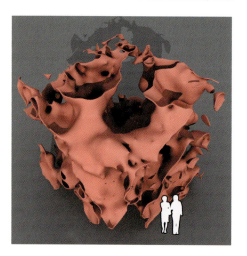

SIMULATION

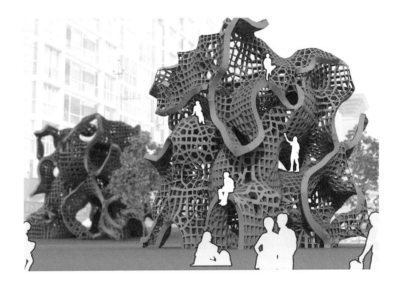

SIMULATION

5.5 TUTORIALS

5.5.1 Tutorial: nCloth for tensile structure – method 1

Designers can use physics as an engine to apply forces to specific Maya objects, including nParticles, nHair, and nCloth. These dynamic objects can be used to simulate physical phenomena. The Nucleus engine provides some specific material parameters, such as stretch resistance, rigidity, and mass, to mimic real-world material properties. This tutorial focuses on a Maya Nucleus simulation in architectural design, which deals with a specific tensile structure.

1. Start with a simple polygon plane to create a radial tent. **Extrude** several faces with the **Division** value of 4. Delete top faces to create openings.

2. Convert the polygon plane into a Maya nCloth. It inherits all the properties of Maya nCloth parameters.

3. Change the **Time Slider** setting in the **Preference** window. Choose **Play Every Frame** in the **Playback Speed** setting. It is important to run the simulation without escaping any frames. When running the animation, the entire nCloth will fall down because the nCloth object has a built-in gravity force. This is different from the Maya particle system, which must be associated with external forces.

4. Create anchor points to pin up the nCloth. Select several points at the corners and convert them by the **Create Transform Constraint** tool. Run the simulation to observe how the flat surface drips and changes into a curved form.

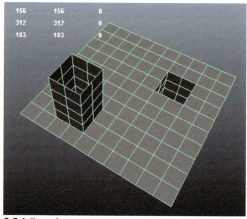

5.5.1 Step 1

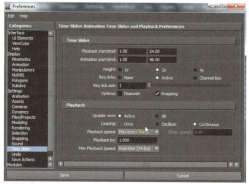

5.5.1 Step 3

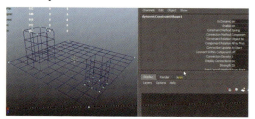

5.5.1 Step 4

5. Open the **Attribute Editor** (**Ctrl + A**) and go to the **Nucleus** tag. Play with the **Gravity** and **Wind** values. The designer can modify these values during the animation play and observe the results in real time.

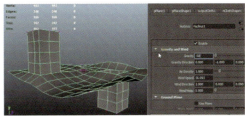

5.5.1 Step 5

6. Go to the **nClothShape** tag in **Attribute Editor** and play with **Stretch Resistance**, **Compression Resistance**, and other **Dynamic Properties**. **The Rest Length Scale** is a property that makes the relaxation effect. The updated results can be observed in real time.

5.5.1 Step 6

5.5.2 Tutorial: nCloth for tensile structure – method 2

1. Create a simple polygon plane. Delete a few faces to create two openings. (For circular openings, project circles onto the mesh and split the mesh with projected curves. Then delete the internal faces).

2. Go to the **nClothShape** tag in **Attribute Editor**. Click the **Presets** button and select an nCloth preset named **RubberSheet**. The preset automatically populates the dynamic properties of the nCloth to simulate this specific material.

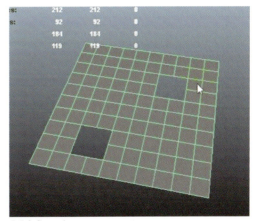

5.5.2 Step 1

3. Create two polygon spheres in the center of the two openings.

4. Create **Transformation Constraints** based on four corner vertices.

5. Select all the eight points along one opening. Hold the **Shift** key to add the sphere into the selection. Click **Component to Component** in the **nConstraint** menu. Repeat this process to create the constraint for the other sphere.

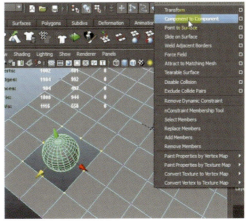

5.5.2 Step 5

105

SIMULATION

6. Animate the sphere. Use the **S** key to keyframe the sphere at frame 1. Move the time slider to frame 300. Move up the sphere to a new position and keyframe the transformation values.

7. Use the same process to animate the other sphere. Move it downwards and keyframe the new position.

8. Play the animation to observe how the nCloth is stretched by the two spheres in different directions and forms a curved radial tent.

9. If selecting **dynamicConstraint** and changing the **Strength** values in the **Attribute Editor** window, the nCloth will be tightened or loosed from the attached spheres.

10. The designer can also select certain edges and use **Convert Polygon Edge to Curve** to generate curves. These curves can be used to create NURBS surfaces or be lofted with pipes.

11. After the nCloth is constructed, if adding on any other operations such as deleting faces, smoothing, or Super Extruding the polygon plane, these modifications will not affect the simulation process since the geometry in the Nucleus solver is still the original model.

5.5.3 Tutorial: Maya Hair and the tensile structure

1. Use the **EP Curve** tool in the top view. Click the start point and the end point to create a straight line.

2. Select the start point of the EP curve and create a **Cluster** from the **Create Deformers** menu in the **Animation** menu group.

5.5.2 Step 6

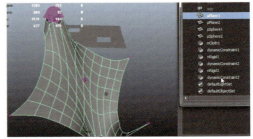
5.5.2 Step 8

5.5.2 Step 9

5.5.2 Step 10

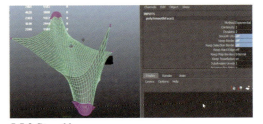
5.5.2 Step 11

106

SIMULATION

3. Select the end point of the EP curve and create another cluster. Both clusters are not visible in the **Outliner** window. When moving any of the two clusters, the straight line will be changed.

4. Use the **Rebuild Curve** tool from the **Edit Curves** menu. In the **Tool Setting** box, set **Number of Spans** to 20, and **Degree** to **3 Cubic**. Now the curve has more points for simulation solver.

5. Select the curve. Click **Make the Selected Curve Dynamic** from the **Hair** menu in the **Dynamics** group.

6. Play the animation. Now the hair is dripped from the middle. In the **Attribute Editor** window, modify the **Forces** in the **hairSystemShape** tag, as well as the **Stiffness** value to adjust the simulation result.

7. Select the hair and use **Revolve** to create a NURBS surface.

8. Because two clusters were created before the curve was rebuilt and converted into nCloth, the designer can modify the curve by moving the cluster after rewinding the timeline to 1. The **revolvedSurface** will update as the designer moves the clusters. Run the simulation again to get the saddled surface.

9. In the history node, change the revolve **Degree** to Linear, **Section** to 6, and **End Sweep** to 180. The Isoparm can also be extruded with a circular profile to create pipes. Run the simulation again to generate the surface.

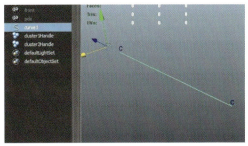

5.5.3 Step 1

5.5.3 Step 4

5.5.3 Step 6

5.5.3 Step 7

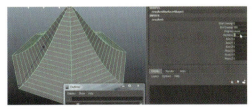

5.5.3 Step 8

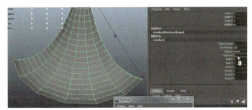

5.5.3 Step 9

107

SIMULATION

6 VISUALIZATION

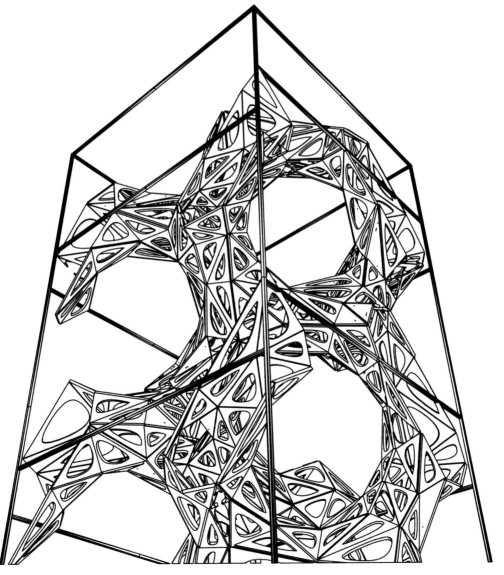

VISUALIZATION

In the contemporary design and build industry, having the ability to explore multiple aspects of design through visual representations is crucial. Designers must learn the tools and methods of conveying a design concept for clear communication. This chapter discusses the basic concepts of visualization through camera, light, material, and rendering, and introduces several efficient methods to produce photo-realistic renderings in Maya.

Tower in Dubai, Tang & Yang Architects. A fish eye camera was used to create the panorama view of the internal structure to achieve an exaggerated effect of the dynamic and intertwined space.

6.1 CAMERA

6.1.1 Camera view

Advanced 3-D programs and rendering engines, through their capacity to apply a virtual camera in a scene, have contributed to the emergence of new methods of form and spatial expression. Simulating and representing a design with 3-D forms, perspective views, animations, and game-like interactive walkthroughs have shifted the emphasis from the conventional illustration and physical-model presentation towards 3-D and animation interpretation. Virtual views through the lens of a virtual camera in 3-D programs are especially effective in generating photo-realistic renderings and walk-in simulations. With the camera tools in the digital environment, it is easy to generate, adjust, and save perspective views that used to be time-consuming to create and difficult to alter by hand.

amount of distortion on the edges of the picture due to the forced perspective projection typical of the wide angle of vision. Besides various camera properties such as focal lenses, depth field, and clipping plan, Maya also provides a target point for the camera, which makes the camera movement and angle control extremely flexible.[2]

6.1.2 Camera lens

The camera lens is an important component in any camera system because it defines the way in which the 3-D world is projected onto the projection plane of a camera. As the focal length of a fixed lens increases, its angle of view decreases. In most 3-D programs, the camera lens can be defined as normal lens, telephoto lens, and wide-angle lens. The normal lens offers a standard human eye 46 degree angle of view. It can fill the field of vision with foreground subjects and background subjects without distorting the perspectives. The telephoto lens has excellent performance for close-up shots. However, it flattens the perceptive and has a narrow angle of view.[1] A wide-angle lens supports a generous 83 degree angle of view. This type of lens provides a small

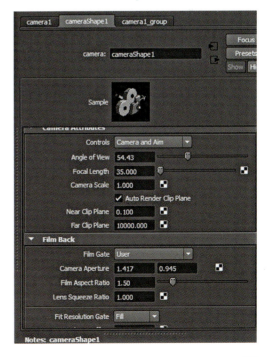

Urban Installations in New York Concourse, Tang & Yang Architects. The design concept was to use kinetic PV panels to capture sunlight during the day and provide lighting to the vegetation during the night. The green vegetation is created by Maya fur. The frame and roof structure supporting PV panels were rendered with Mental Ray skylight in Maya (top). The night time rendering highlights the possible effect on the vegetation planted on the vertical walls (bottom).

6. 2 LIGHTING

6.2.1 Light properties

For architectural and interior design, light is an extremely important design component that can change the perception of a scene as much as the objects themselves. Light in a computer-generated scene simulates the lighting principles in the physical world. The simulation must account for the type of the light source, its color, intensity, attenuation, and shadow.[3] In the physical world, the illumination of a scene has more than one hue. For instance, household incandescent light bulbs emit light that is tinted slightly yellow. Daylight is typically a mixture of blue color diffuse light from the sky and orange light from the sun. The intensity of a light decreases as the distance to the light increases. As light radiates from a point, illumination attenuates in an inverse square pattern. With inverse square falling off, the intensity of the light controls the size of the area it makes visibly. A brighter light illuminates a bigger part of the scene. If a light is very dim, it can only brighten a small area and quickly ceases to be visible.

6.2.2 Shadow

Light can cast shadows to add realism to the rendering. Most of the rendering programs support two types of shadow: depth map shadow and ray-traced shadow.

A depth map shadow, also called shadow map, uses a light's point of view to determine where shadows will be rendered in a 3-D program. Depth map shadow is usually adjustable with the shadow map size or resolution settings. Increasing the resolution of a shadow map can result in sharper and more accurate shadows, although that also increases the rendering time.

Ray-traced shadow computes the path of light rays to produce accurate shadows. The shadow cast by a transparent object appears lighter than the shadow cast by an opaque object. Rendering each point of a scene with ray-traced shadows requires extensive computation of the light and the point being rendered. This process can be time consuming for a complex scene with many transparent objects. Therefore, a ray-traced shadow often takes longer to render than a depth-map shadow takes.

In an architectural rendering, designers can use the three-point lighting method, which is widely used in photography, to set up the basic lighting environment.[4] Single shadow casting from the key light, such as sunlight, is typical for setting up primary lighting without building up any complexity.[5] In the physical world, light reflects among surfaces. No shadow is completely dark. Therefore, in rendering programs, a fill light needs be set up to simulate the indirect light in a shadow area. Since rendering programs provide the option to turn on or turn off the shadows of a light, designers can turn on the shadows from the key light, but turn off the shadows from the fill light.

6.2.3 Light and vertex color

Baking light information into vertex color is a popular technique widely used in the game industry. Instead of rendering lighting effects based on the light parameters, this process relies on the vertex points within the mesh to save color and lighting values. There are four vertex color values including red, green, blue channels, as well as alpha channel. Vertex color can be either painted manually or baked directly from lightings or shaders in Maya. The objects, with the embedded vertex color values, can be imported into other real-time

Rabbit model lighting. A red light from the top and a blue light from the bottom were mixed on the surface of two rabbit models. One rabbit is high polygon model and the other is low polygon model. The lights and shadows were baked into vertex colors.

environments such as a scene generated by game engines. This prelighting process is efficient in the real-time rendering environment because objects can be illuminated without time-consuming calculations in real time. Compared with rendering objects with standard lighting setups, the graphic processing unit (GPU) can handle vertex color much faster and create a higher frame rate for interactive video games. However, the color per vertex data are limited by the positions of vertices and do not provide the same quality as standard rendering.

Because the vertex color values are stored on the vertex level, designers can extract information stored in the RGB + alpha channels and transfer it across various programs. For example, the solar analysis data can be captured into vertex colors and be used to manipulate the topology of window panels. Designers can even bake the lighting information, structural performance, or simulated acoustic data into vertex colors and use them to control the design.

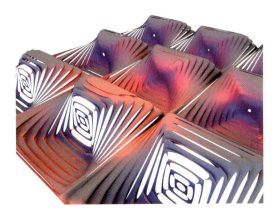

Bake lighting information into the geometry. In this case, the red and blue vertex colors were baked with two Omni lights in Maya. The model was transferred to Rhino and Grasshopper afterwards to control the geometry parametrically according to the vertex color. The opening dimension of each rib on the surface was driven by the vertex color in that specific location.

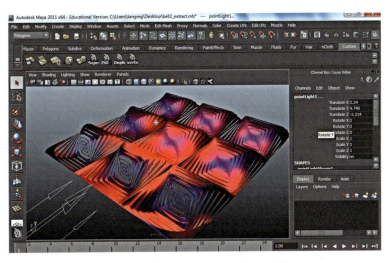

VISUALIZATION

6.2.4 Tutorial: Bake Maya lighting into vertex color

1. Create a polygon in Maya.

2. Create two **Omni Lights**, each with a different color. The polygon is now illuminated by two different colors based on its orientation and distance to the lights. The designer can change one of the **Omni Lights** to **Directional Light** and observe a different result. Pay attention to the darkness, hue, and blending of colors across various surfaces.

3. Bake the lighting effect into vertex color by using the **Batch Bake (Mental Ray)** tool. Check the **Bake to Vertices** option.

4. The designer should see the vertex color embedded in the surface. Even after deleting the lights, the surface color is still visible.

5. Use the **Extract** tool to break the polygon into several pieces. A small offset value can be defined to create gaps between each piece.

6. Use **Combine** to merge these pieces into one polygon mesh.

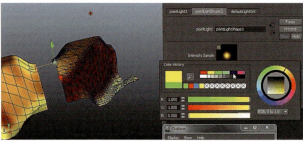

6.2.4 Step 2

6.2.4 Step 3

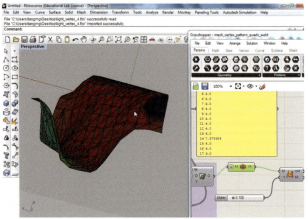

6.2.4 Step 9

116

VISUALIZATION

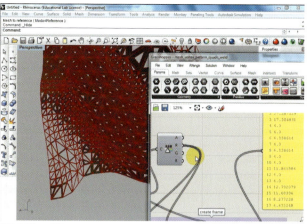

6.2.4 Step 10

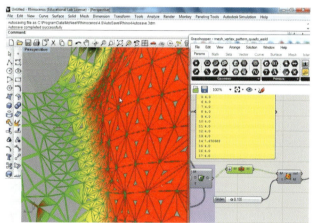

6.2.4 Step 10

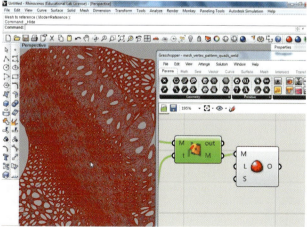

6.2.4 Step 11

7. Export the polygon mesh as **FBX** format and bring it into Rhino program.

8. Rhino reads the vertex color computed originally in Maya.

9. Grasshopper scripts can be used to extract the vertex color and execute other operations.

10. Create a frame structure based on the mesh. The sizes of openings are driven by the red color values of each face.

11. Weld the vertex to fill their gaps. Smooth the entire mesh into a perforated amorphous surface.

117

6.3 MATERIAL

6.3.1 Shader and materials

In the digital design environment, computer graphics can simulate the materiality of an object by applying material or shader. The same object can appear to be made of wood, glass, or brick by mapping actual images of these materials onto the surface. A shader is a collection of surface characteristics and shading techniques that are applied to an object during the rendering process. The basic surface characteristics contained in most shaders include color, reflectivity, and transparency. Many 3-D programs provide a material editor to control the values of these attributes to simulate the characteristics of a specific material.

Rendering of Ronchamp Church. Modeled by Maya polygon tools. Various concrete images were modified in Photoshop and mapped to the model to simulate colors and textures. Techniques includings UV wrapping projection, BUMP material, and HDRI lighting were used to create the final photorealistic rendering.

6.3.2 Maya shader network

Maya shader network is a collection of rendering nodes, including material nodes, texture nodes, and utility nodes, which can be connected by manipulating the Hypershade window. [6] Maya also provides a wide range of material editing tools and can simulate a variety of material effects. Its unique Mental Ray material, multilayer shader, and procedural texture provide an advanced node-based shader network. [7] Map channels allow designers to easily compose a shader with customized diffuse color, reflection, self-illumination, and bump effects. Its displacement map is a fast way to render realistic 3-D effects from 2-D textures. The UV mapping tools allow designers to unwrap complex geometries with an appropriate UV projection.

Place2dtexture node is one of the most important utility nodes in the Maya shader network. It can be used to change the texture properties such as Offset, Repeat UV, and Rotate UV. [8] Designers can also use a single Place2dtexture node to simultaneously control multiple channels such as color, bump, or transparent channels, to provide a matching effect among textures from various channels.

6.3.3 Procedural texture vs. bitmap texture

Procedural texture, such as fractal and noise, is different from a bitmap image because it is generated by a mathematical algorithm and computed by several parameters in real time with infinite resolution. Its pattern can be modified by changing the parameters such as frequency and magnitude. This kind of texture is often used together with advanced displacement map to create procedural terrain or abstract sculptures.

6.3.4 Map/channel

The term *channel* is interchangeable with *map*. A 2-D image file can be connected in a shader network to simulate texture and material attributes such as reflectivity and roughness. Channels can modulate the look of a surface by linking the color value of the texture to the surface where that texture is mapped. Different image maps can also be combined to control different aspects of the surface characteristics. The types of channels covered in this chapter include color, bump, transparency, reflection, and self-illumination channels.

6.3.5 Color map/channel

Color maps are also called *picture maps*, *diffuse maps*, or *texture maps*, because they often involve photographic images with a fixed number of pixels and a finite resolution. [9] Distinctive color maps often have a significant influence on the overall appearance of an object, especially when viewed from a distance.

6.3.6 Bump map/channel

Bump maps are powerful in simulating the roughness or bumpiness of a 3-D surface. By altering the normal direction of the surface during the rendering process, bump maps can simulate surface relief based on Alpha Gain value. The darker colors in a bump map represent depressions, while the lighter colors represent elevations.

6.3.7 Transparency map/channel

A monochromatic 2-D image can be used as a transparency map to define the opacity of a 3-D object. The brightness value of the pixels in a transparency map is used to determine whether the surface will be transparent, opaque, or translucent. A transparency map can be used as a clip map to create the appearance of cutouts on an object. A completely white area of a clip map will hide the corresponding part of an object to create the illusion that the pattern has been cut out from the surface of the object. This technique is also called the *billboard method*.[10]

Designers can take advantage of Maya's Transparency channel to create the mask effect. An alpha channel TGA or TIFF image can be used to control the visibility of a shader.[11] Instead of modeling in details, a complex form can be visualized by using transparency map, which significantly speeds up the rendering process. By using a transparency map, designers can easily adjust a location and repetition pattern. The rendering result is highly effective when designers combine a transparency map with a bump map to reinforce each other. For instance, window frames with complex profiles can be rendered by adding a 2-D bump map rather than modeling 3-D frames, while the transparent glass openings can be rendered with a transparency map. However, since this mask technique does not generate geometric thickness, the openings and voids will appear flat if the camera is moved close to the window. Therefore, this technique should only be used to render objects in distance.

Fractal Salon-A temporary outdoor gallery space, MadCubic. The project is thus named because the pattern of the building skin was generated by fractal algorithms and then projected onto the roof and façades. An alpha channel image was used to render the perforated panels.

VISUALIZATION

6.3.8 Reflection map/channel

Reflection maps are often used to simulate highly reflective and polished surfaces such as metal and glass. An image can be projected as the reflection map. Compared to calculating the actual 3-D environment reflections using ray tracing, using a "fake" reflection map that can mimic actual reflections takes less rendering time. However, designers should use the true reflection when accurate reflections are required, such as rendering reflections in a mirror.

6.3.9 Self-illumination map/channel

Light-emitting materials can be achieved through map channels called the *Ambient channel* and *Incandescence channel*. When a non-black color or an image is attached to these channels, the material appears bright and to be emitting illumination. In this situation, even if there are no Maya lights, a bright self-illuminated object, such as a neon sign, can still be rendered with these channels. If the object was assigned with glowing effect, designers can simulate bleeding lighting patterns without actually creating any Maya lights.

6.4 SPECIAL RENDER NODES

6.4.1 Ambient occlusion

Maya Mental Ray renderer offers ambient occlusion as a special node. Ambient occlusion calculates the illumination of dark areas based on how much indirect lighting is blocked by a nearby object. The calculation is performed by emitting rays from each point on the surface and testing how visible the point is from the sky dome. The brightness of a point is determined by how much shadow that point receives. If the surface is a concave shape, like a gap, it gets less light and appears darker, while a convex shape gets more lights and appears brighter. Instead of rendering the full material and lighting effects, ambient occlusion renders objects with white material and emulates an overcast sky. It is an effective rendering method to visualize complex forms and illustrate spatial relationships among them.[12]

When applying multilayer rendering, ambient occlusion can be added as a rendering layer and later be composed with other renderings. Designers can compose diffuse rendering, reflection

Interlocking Tower, eVolo Skyscraper Design Competition, Tang & Yang Architects and MadCubic. Instead of creating interior lighting features of the tower, a 2-D image was used to create a self-illumination pattern. This spatial material was mapped to selected parts of the building skin to achieve the lighting result.

121

VISUALIZATION

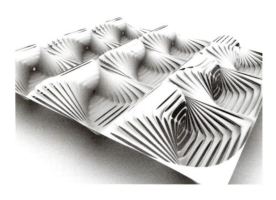

rendering, shadow rendering, and ambient occlusion and control them independently. The benefit is that designers can effectively alter them later with image-editing programs that provide more flexible control of the hue, saturation, or brightness for each layer. Ambient occlusion can also be baked into vertex color, which can be transferred to other 3-D programs. Designers can extract RGB values from the vertex color and use them to manipulate the object and create tessellations.

6.4.2 Soft edge shader

Another useful shader is the Mental Ray soft edge shader, with which designers can create the radius bevel edge effect around a sharp corner without having to model the beveled edge. Because of its significant benefit in saving the modeling and rendering time, this special shader is a good method when working with smooth corner geometries such as with furniture.

6.4.3 Ramp color

Ramp color can illustrate gradient changes across a surface. It can be used to represent a topographic map, the curvature of a surface, or other data distributed across the surface. Designers can also control the surface tessellations based on the ramp color.

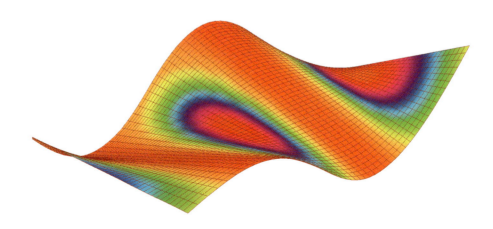

VISUALIZATION

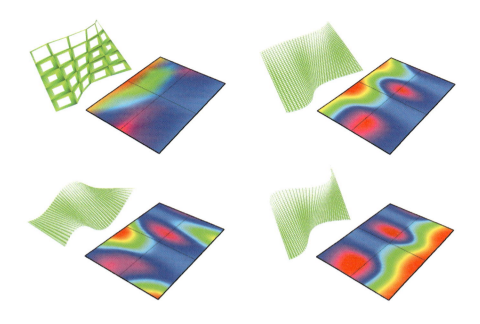

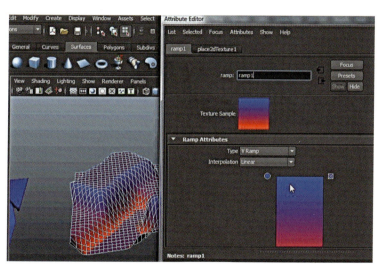

6.5 PROJECTION

6.5.1 Projection types

Projection is a method to wrap a 2-D image around an object.[13] There are many projection types in Maya; some are simple while others are complex.

Planar projection applies textures on planar surfaces and is projected onto an object. It is common to project an image to a surface that is parallel to the projection plan. For example, designers can use planar projection to put a billboard image on a building façade or a door panel.

Cubic projection is a variation of planar projection. It projects a texture onto each side of a box. This projection can be used effectively to apply textures to both rectangular and curved objects. In Maya, cubic projection is called *tri-planar* projection, which takes the X, Y, and Z axes simultaneously to create three planar projections surrounding an object. For the cubicle architectural form, this is the common projection method for adding surface material. After applying tri-planar projection, the designer can generate a projection placement node for interactive manipulation. The interactive placement node is a selectable object in the Maya Outliner window. It can be modified as a regular object and manipulated by transforming tools. The transformation of the placement node affects the materials on all objects to which the node has been assigned.

Cylindrical projection applies textures to surfaces by wrapping the texture image around a cylinder until the two ends of the image meet on the object. This projection technique is useful for applying materials around columns.

Spherical projection applies a texture image by wrapping it around a sphere. It is useful to project maps onto round objects such as domes.

UV projection allows textures be stretched for a good fit and be associated with a vertex component in a polygon model. UV projection coordinates pixels in the 2-D texture and marks the corresponding vertices on the mesh. UV texture mapping tools and UV texture editor in Maya are

Green Harbor Design of Nordhavene in Norway, Tang & Yang Architects. To efficiently visualize a large 3-D urban model, various materials were projected onto the low polygon urban model to represent architectural details such as windows, balconies, and green spaces on the roofs. Because the model was designed for rendering in real time with Xbox XNA game engine, it was essential to control the number of polygon faces in the scene. A high frame rate is achieved by using various materials and projections to provide architectural details.

based on this projection concept, which allow designers to manipulate textures per UV point.

Depending on the relationship between the texture and the corresponding object, multiple projections are generally used together. Designers can select a particular face and apply a specific projection type to achieve the best result. The previous projections are always accessible under the history INPUTS node. Therefore, designers can easily revisit these projections and manipulate them.

Customize the projection. The building facades and roof were painted as one image in Photoshop and wrapped around the 3-D model in Maya. This technique allows designers to fully control the irregular textures and shapes.

6.5.2 Tutorial: Texture mapping

1. Create a cube and attach a **Lambert** shader to it. Attach a texture file to the color channel.

2. Select a group of faces on the cube and apply the **Planar map** tool. Pick one axis from **X**, **Y**, **Z** axes in the tool setting box. The designer should see the projection manipulator directly in the 3-D view.

3. Scale, rotate, or move the projection manipulator and observe how the texture is updated on the faces.

4. Continue step 2 and apply a different projection to a different face group.

5. The designer can hold right mouse button over the object and choose an existing projection name in the pop-up menu and reactive its manipulator.

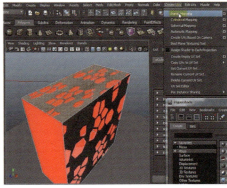

6.5.2 Step 2

6.5.2 Step 3

6.5.2 Step 3

6.5.2 Step 5

6.5.2 Step 5

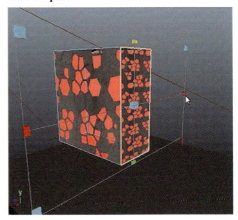

VISUALIZATION

6.5.3 Tutorial: Tri-planar projection

1. Create multiple objects and assign a shader to all of them.

2. In the shader's **Attribute** window, click the shader's **Color** channel and attach a **Projection** node to it.

3. Choose **Tri-planar** from the drop down menu within the **Projection** node's **Attribute Editor** window.

4. Attach an image file to the **Image** channel in the Tri-planar's **Attribute Editor** window.

5. Now the graph network will display a projection node between the image node and the final shader node.

6. Do a test rendering and the designer should see all the objects assigned with this shader will share the same Tri-planar projection. If a new object is created and assigned the existing shader, it will automatically inherit the same projection as other objects.

7. To manipulate the Tri-planar projection directly, the designer can choose the **Fit to Box** option to create a gizmo in the scene. The gizmo object can be manipulated directly by using Move, Rotate, or Scale tools.

8. The Tri-planar projection can be applied to a NURBS surface. It will override the NURBS surface's internal UV mapping.

6.5.3 Step 2

6.5.3 Step 3

6.5.3 Step 5

6.5.3 Step 7

VISUALIZATION

6.5.4 Tutorial: Creating details with texture mapping

1. Create a box.

2. Open the **Hypershade** window. Create a **Blinn** shader.

3. Attach a concrete image to the blinn shader's **Color** channel.

4. Use the **place2dtexture** node to adjust the texture scale.

5. Assign the blinn shader to the box. Press 7 on the keyboard to display the texture. Now the designer should be able to see the concrete texture on the box.

6. Open the concrete image in Photoshop. Create a new alpha channel and a black-and-white pattern in that channel. Save the file as TGA format.

7. Update the texture file link to the new TGA file in Maya. The designer should see part of the box become transparent. The transparency is driven by the black-and-white image in the alpha channel in the TGA file.

8. Go back to Photoshop. Update the black-and-white pattern and add some gray color shapes. Resave the TGA file. The gray color will later be rendered as semi-translucent materials in Maya.

9. Click the **Reload** button to update the texture image in Maya.

10. Set up a light inside of the box. Turn on the **Ray Tracing** option in the Light Attribute window. Turn on the **Ray Tracing** option in the Render Attributes window as well and do a test rendering. Now

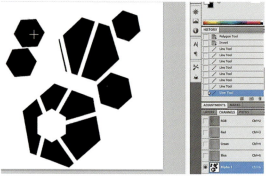

6.5.4 Step 6

6.5.4 Step 7

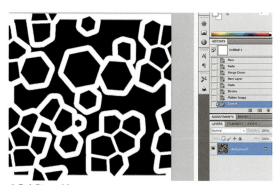

6.5.4 Step 11

6.5.4 Step 14

128

the designer should see the shadow casted from the transparent openings across the box surface.

11. Create another black-and-white image with certain patterns in the alpha channel. Save it as another TGA file and update the link in Maya blinn shader to this new file.

12. Create black-and-white boundary lines surrounding all the openings to mimic window frames. Save the new file as JPEG format. There is no alpha channel in this file format.

13. Attach the black-and-white image to the **Bump** channel of the same blinn shader. Make sure the **place2dtexture** node in bump channel has the same setting as the color channel.

14. The bump values can be adjusted by double clicking the bump node in the **Hypershade** window.

15. Do a test rendering to observe the 3D bump effect surrounding all the openings.

Tower Museum, New York City, Tang & Yang Architects. To create a rough texture across the building units, the noise procedural texture in Maya was used to create the bump texture, which was reinforced by the reflective lighting effect to simulate the metal material.

VISUALIZATION

6.5.5 Tutorial: Ambient occlusion rendering

1. Create several objects in Maya and assign a **surface shader** to all of them.

2. In the **Hypershade** window, choose a Mental Ray Texture named *Mib_amb_occlusion* and connect it to the surface shader.

3. Now all objects are black color. Set **Render Using** to **mental ray** rendering in the **Render Settings** window. Do a test rendering to get a rough ambient occlusion effect.

4. Adjust the quality of ambient occlusion. Double click the **Mib_amb_occlusion** node and open its **Attribute Editor** window. Change the **Sample** from 16 to 64. Another test rendering shows the ambient occlusion is smoother and more accurate.

5. In the **Rendering Settings** window, set **Image Size** to a higher resolution in the **Common** tag. Set **Quality Preset** to **Production** rendering quality in the **Quality** tag, which results in a longer time for rendering. Save the final image as TIFF format.

6. Now compose the ambient occlusion style with other rendering styles. Set a new blinn shader and assign it to all objects. Create a Mental Ray **Physical Sun and Sky** in the **Indirect Lighting** tag. A direction light named *sunDirection* will be automatically created by Maya. Click the **Render the current frame** button and render the scene. Save the rendering as a TIFF image.

7. Change the *sunDirection* light angle and render another lighting condition. Save the image as TIFF format.

8. Compose all three TIFF images in Photoshop, one ambient occlusion and two Mental Ray skylight renderings. The designer can also use the alpha channel provided by TIFF to compose a sky background.

6.5.5 Step 2

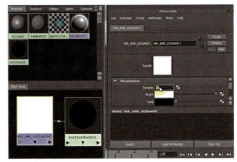
6.5.5 Step 4

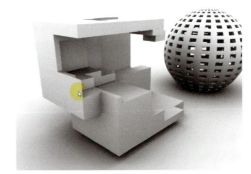
6.5.5 Step 5

6.5.5 Step 8

6.5.6 Tutorial: Reflection map and self-illumination material

1. Create a simple Maya scene with a few objects.

2. Create a **blinn** shader and assign it to the objects.

3. Attach a sky image to the **Reflection** channel. Now the image is rendered in the reflection.

4. Attach a black-and-white checker image to the **Ambient** channel. A procedural **checker** texture in Maya can also be used and attached to the **Ambient** channel. Do a test rendering to see the result.

5. Use the middle mouse button to drag the same checker node to the shader and link it to the **Incandescence** channel. Check the **Glowing Effect** option in the **Special Effects** tag. Do a test rendering to observe the white light bleeding from the white patterns.

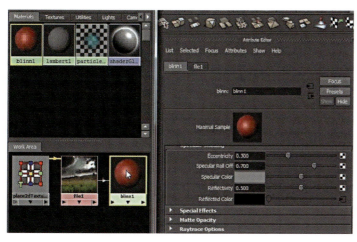

6.5.6 Step 3

6.5.6 Step 5

VISUALIZATION

6. 6 RENDERING

Maya provides four rendering engines: hardware rendering, software rendering, vector rendering, and Mental Ray rendering. Maya hardware rendering is usually used to render particle systems. Software rendering is the default engine to render ray tracing and non-global illumination renderings.[14] Designers can apply Maya vector rendering to generate vector-format graphics such as hidden line style images. Mental Ray rendering provides global illumination (GI) with features such as Final Gathering and Photon maps.[15] The high dynamic range (HDR) image-based rendering has become a popular variation of GI in recent years. HDR image-based rendering extracts global illumination information by analyzing photographic data. HDR photography is used to capture the full range of illumination and recreate the light source in 3-D environment.

Wireframe rabbit. A hidden line style rabbit can be rendered with several options including Maya vector rendering, Maya Toon shader, or Mental Ray contour. Maya vector rendering is the ideal choice to create a clean vector image.

It is critical to compare different rendering settings and understand their effect on rendering time. Here are a few examples of testing for a simple scene with various rendering methods. Some methods can be used in conjunction to create images that can be composed as multiple passes in image editing programs.

Mathematical sculpture. In order to visualize the interlocking effect of exterior and interior surfaces, the digital light needs to be computed to travel and bounce inside of the model. A HDR skylight, Photon mapping, and Global Illumination were used to achieve the final result.

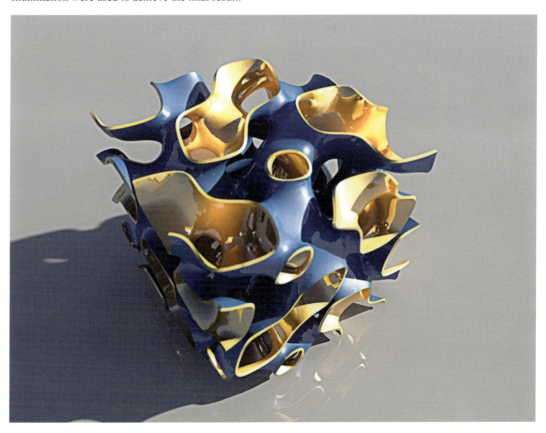

Ray Tracing
Rendering time: 2:04

Ray Tracing
Rendering time: 2:13
Ray radius: 30, Shadow Rays: 12

Raycasting with Depth Shadow
Rendering time: 0:41
Shadow map res: 1024, Filter: 6

Raycasting with Depth Shadow
Rendering time: 0:12
Shadow map res: 1024, Filter: 4

Mental Ray GI
Rendering time: 3:11
Accuracy: 1000, Radius: 24
Photon Inten: 80000, Photon: 100000

Mental Ray GI
Rendering time: 13:12
Accuracy: 6000, Radius: 400
Photon Inten: 80000, Photon: 100000

Mental Ray Final Gathering
Rendering time: 2:01
Accuracy: 100
Max Radius: 20, Min Radius: 2

Final Gathering + Ray Tracing
Rendering time: 3:14
Accuracy: 500
Max Radius: 20, Min Radius: 2

6.6.1 Image composite

Image compositing combines several different renderings into one. A complex 3-D scene can be rendered in layers. Different objects in the scene can be put into different rendering layers. Maya also provides multi-render passes to render shadow, reflection, and other passes separately. These passes can be composed by image editing. The passes and layers are batch rendered and saved as TIFF or TGA formats in Maya to preserve the alpha channel, and then composed in the image editing programs.

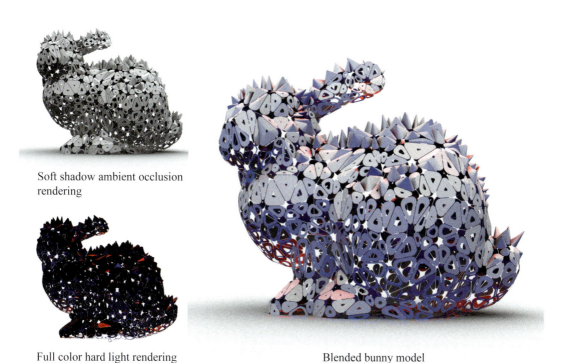

Soft shadow ambient occlusion rendering

Full color hard light rendering

Blended bunny model

Composing of a bunny model. The multi-pass rendering generates a full color hard light rendering and a soft shadow ambient occlusion rendering. These two renderings were blended in Photoshop to demonstrate how the lighting color can parametrically drive the tessellation pattern.

VISUALIZATION

6.6.2 Tutorial: Multiple layer rendering

1. Set **render layers** and move selected objects into each layer.

2. Click the **Render Settings** button in the render layers. Right click **Render Using** text and choose **Create Layer Override** in the pop-up menu. Define different rendering engines in different render layers. For example, set one layer as **Mental Ray render**, another layer as **Maya vector rendering**, and so on.

6.6.2 Step 2

3. Create a new rendering layer. Right click the layer and choose **Attributes** in the pop-up menu. In the Layer's **Attributes Editor** window, left click the **Preset** button and choose **Occlusion**. Now this render layer is automatically set as this special rendering style. The designer should notice all objects in that render layer are assigned with a surface shader and turned into black color.

6.6.2 Step 3

4. In the **Render Settings** window of the **Master render** layer, click the **Create Render Passes** button in the **Passes** Tag and set multiple **render passes**.

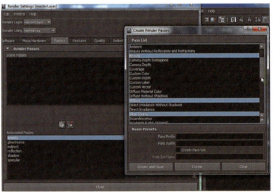

6.6.2 Step 4

5. In the master render layer's **Render Settings** window, set image format to TIFF, and resolution to high with production quality. If multiple frames in Maya timeline will be rendered, the designer needs to define the **Frame Range**.

6. Use **Batch Rendering** in Maya **Render** menu to execute all rendering tasks.

7. Browse the destination folder and compose the images in Photoshop.

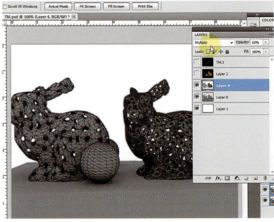

6.6.2 Step 7

136

ANIMATION

7 ANIMATION

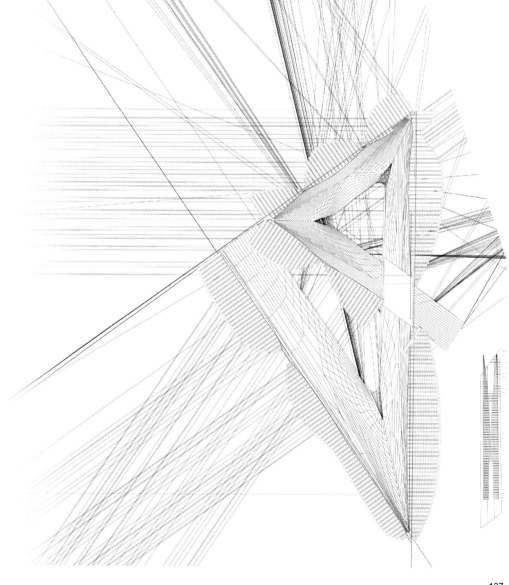

7.1 ANIMATION AS VISUALIZATION TOOL

Computer animation is the technique of creating moving illusion in computers. The architecture profession has embraced the animation field because it is a powerful tool to visualize and communicate 3-D forms. Design 3-D animation requires the ability to think in four dimensions: three spatial dimensions and one temporal dimension. There are various 3-D animation techniques in the visual arts industry, such as keyframe animation, morphing animation, kinematics animation, and particle animation. Animating a camera along a motion path is most commonly employed by architects to create a cinematic fly-through. Compared with traditional physical models, fly-through animation can simulate the experience of moving through a space.[1] Architects also use animation to simulate the changing spatial features, such as the changing light attributes including position, angle, color, and intensity.[2]

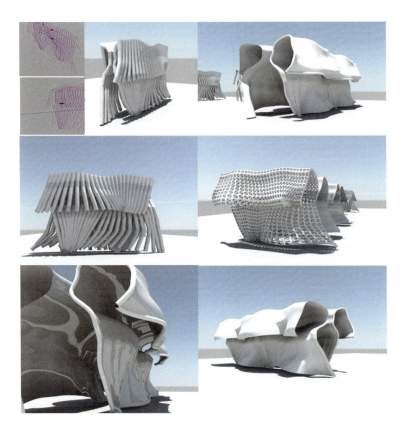

7.2 ANIMATION AS A MODELING TOOL

In Maya, animated objects can be frozen into a sequence of static forms that can be subsequently integrated into the form-making process. For instance, designers can animate a beam flying through the space that gradually changes its dimensions and proportions as it flies. The Maya animation Snapshot tool can be used to duplicate the beam along the timeline and freeze these changing values into a series of static forms.

Designers can also create a cluster deformer node to group several CV points. The cluster's translation, rotation, and scale attributes can be keyframed. Its changing transformation attributes will affect each CV point within the set. As regular elements visible in the Outliner window, the formation channels of a cluster are accessible and can be keyframed along the timeline.

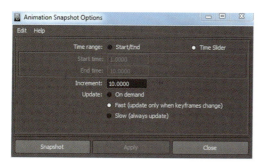

7.2.1 Animation of CV

Other than the parameters on the object level such as the transformation attributes, designers can also animate on the control vertices (CVs) level.[3] For instance, a Maya curve includes several CV points whose base values become accessible in the Transformation channels when selected. Designers can change the CV points' X, Y, and Z values directly and keyframe them along the timeline to create an animation.

ANIMATION

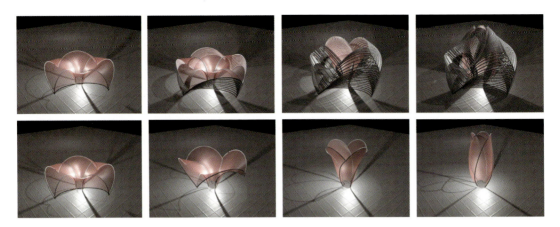

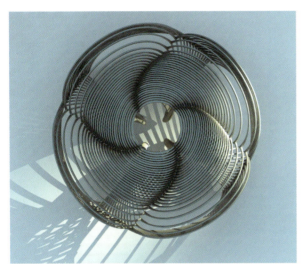

Blooming Architecture: A New Monument in Miami, the second place, Miami monument design competition, Tang & Yang Architects.

Inspired by the rhythm of motion graphics and the abstract expression painting, this project studied how motion could be frozen into a static form. It is the collapse of time into the present, the transparency of processes – the way in which the viewer can so readily reconstruct the act of creation – gives the drip paintings an extraordinary immediacy.

The monument is a representation of the blooming of Miami. Animation techniques were used to inhabit the duration of time into the present. The form of the monument was shaped through the simulation of a blooming flower. Each steel structure member was generated by capturing the motion of a flower's blooming sequence and then transformed into a static architectural form by Maya.

ANIMATION

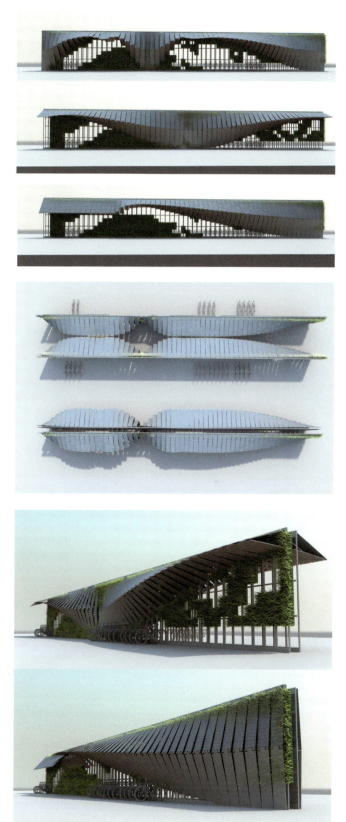

Bicycle Booth. The form of the booth is generated by Maya animation tools.

141

ANIMATION

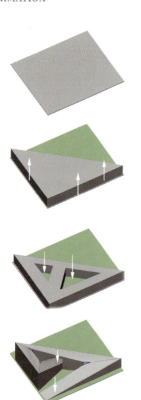

Dallas Eye, Special award, Urban Revision: Dallas competition, Tang & Yang Architects.

This project explored design strategies to develop the site into a dense, vibrant, and dynamic city block, which in the meanwhile was also a self-sufficient agriculture base supporting its own population.

A series of small scale vertical farms were proposed, integrated with food markets, public transportations, bike sharing facilities, graffiti walls, and other civil facilities. By changing the relationships among individual ribs, the vertical farms could perform various scenarios and respond to various plants' needs. Similar as human's eye lip, the kinetic PV panels installed on the top ribs served as the secondary skin, which could open and close according to internal functionalities and external environmental factors (created by Maya animation tools). By reconfiguring the angles of each rib, this secondary skin can be converted into exhibition spaces, walls for graffiti art, or bicycle parking spaces during the winter time.

ANIMATION

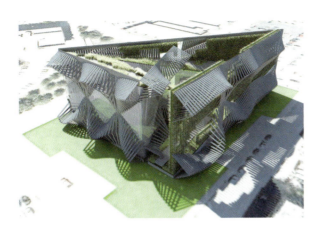

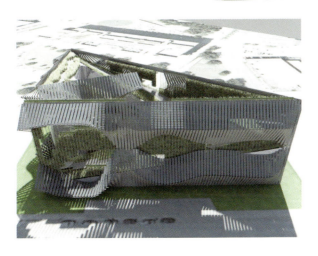

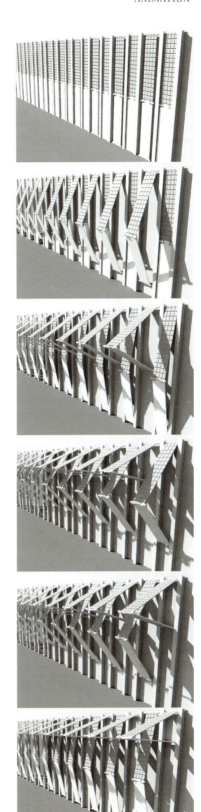

143

ANIMATION

7.2.2 Deformation animation

Maya deformation tools, such as Sculpt deformer, Lattice deformer, Wrap deformer, and Non-linear Bend deformer, allow designers to deform objects by interactive handles. Just like regular animations, designers can keyframe the deformation handles to create deformation animation. For instance, designers can apply a lattice deformer to deform an object by manipulating selected lattice points. The selected lattice points can also be grouped as a cluster to create a keyframe animation. Animation snapshots can be used to freeze the deformation animation along the timeline.

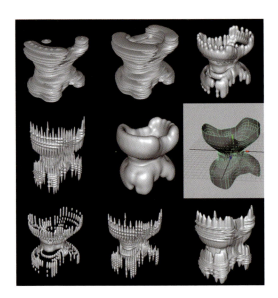

Soft manipulation can be used to create deformations as well. By applying the Soft Modification tool, Maya will create a special deformer called *softModHandel*. This deformer includes attributes such as Falloff Radius and Falloff Curve, which can be animated to create ripple effects.

values are keyframed in the timeline, the animation can generate all the transitional values in between. Designers can then bake animated forms by animation snapshot at the end.

7.2.3 Animate the history nodes

Most actions in Maya will be recorded as history INPUTS nodes, which are available in the Attribute Editor and the Channel Box. Animation can be applied to the parameters embedded in the history nodes. For instance, the INPUTS node of a polygon cube includes attributes such as width, height, depth, and subdivisions. These numeric values can be animated over time by setting up keyframes. The INPUTS node also contains previous operations applied to the object. As long as the attributes are numeric, designers can keyframe them to create animation. For example, the chamfer operation has a value between 0 and 0.5, and the Blend operation controls the morphing weight between 0 and 1. Once these changing

7.2.4 Animation through motion path

Besides creating fly-through animation, the motion-path method can be used with an animation snapshot to create models with repetitive components. For instance, designers can define a curve as a motion path, group vertices in a truss model as a cluster, and attach the cluster to the motion path. An animation snapshot of the motion path will generate a series of structure members.

7.2.5 Animation through parent/child relationship

If an animation for an object has already been created, and another new object is designed to follow the existing animated object, designers can simply attach the new

144

object as the child of the animated object to create a constant spatial relationship between these two objects. By doing so, the two objects will always move together in the animation. For example, to create the effect that the moon moves in a circular pattern around the earth, and they both move together in a circular pattern around the sun, designers can attach the moon object to a circular animation path, and then attach the animation path as a child object to the earth object. The earth object can be animated along another circular path surrounding the sun.

7.2.6 Animation through simulation

Instead of manually controlling the movement of objects, designers can set up forces, such as gravity or newton field, and animate objects by the simulation of physical phenomena. Assigning collisions, constraints, or other properties to objects can simulate complex interactions among these objects. Such simulation can also be integrated with other common animation techniques in Maya. For instance, designers can set up the nCloth to simulate a fabric tensile structure; the transform constraints of nCloth can be animated to stretch and deform the fabric.

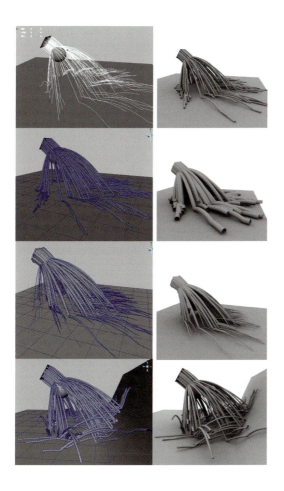

Powerful Maya animation tools allow designers to animate many attributes of an object over time. Keyframe animation, path animation, motion-capture animation, simulation, as well as skeleton and joint animation offer designers the freedom to manipulate objects in various ways. The animation snapshot allows designers to freeze any changes along the timeline into a sequence of static objects. These animation tools have offered architecture and interior designers a host of new creative possibilities.

ANIMATION

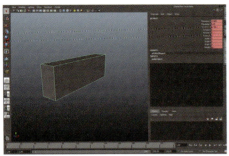

7.3.1 Step 1

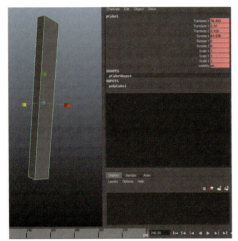

7.3.1 Step 3

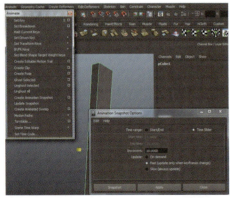

7.3.1 Step 5

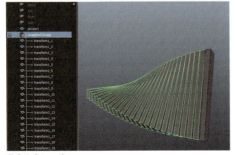

7.3.1 Step 6

7.3 TUTORIALS

7.3.1 Tutorial: Keyframe animation

1. Create a polygon cube. Set the timeline to 240 frames.

2. Select the cube. Use the **S** key to key frame the transformation attributes in frame 0. Now the channel values are displayed as red color.

3. Move the timeline to frame 240. Select the cube and manipulate its transformation values such as **Translate, Move**, or **Scale**. Use the **S** key to save these new values. Play the animation and the cube should be animated along the timeline.

4. Additional key frames can be added in the timeline. The animation will update according to the new key frames.

5. Go to the **Animate** menu under the **Animation** group, and choose **Create Animation Snapshot**. Open the tool setting box. Change the **Time Range** to **Time Slider**, and **Increment** to 10, which will create a duplication every 10 frames.

6. Open the **Outliner** window. Select the snapshot1Group object and move it away from the original animated object. Open the group node and the designer should see 24 objects inside.

7. If updating the original object's keyframe by pressing the **S** key to record the change, all 24 objects within the group node will automatically update.

8. Delete the snapshot1Group object and redo the **Create Animation Snapshot** with **Increment** set to 2. Now 120 objects are created under the group node.

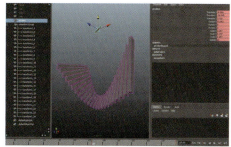

7.3.1 Step 7

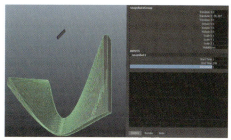

7.3.1 Step 8

7.3.2 Tutorial: Motion path animation

1. Create a polygon cube and a curve. Select both objects and choose **Attach to Motion Path** from the **Animate > Motion Paths** menu. Play the animation and observe how the polygon cube is flowing along the curve.

2. Select several vertices and manipulate the cube. Use **Create Animation Snapshot** with **Increment** set to 2. Click the **Apply** button and thus generate 120 cubes.

3. Edit the curve with CV points. Once choosing **Update Motion Trail > Snapshot**, the 120 cubes will automatically update to reflect the change.

7.3.2 Step 1

7.3.2 Step 2

ANIMATION

7.3.3 Tutorial: Animation on object level and component level

1. Create an **EP curve** with **Curve degree** set to **1 linear**. Draw the curve in the front view.

2. Select all the CV points and press the **S** key to key frame their values. Click the frame 240 in the **Time Slider**. Select CV points and move them into a new location. Press the **S** key again to record these new transformation values. Play the animation to see how the curve is morphing to a different shape.

3. Click the first frame in **Time Slider**, select the entire curve object and press the **S** key to keyframe its transformation values.

4. Click frame 240 in **Time Slider**. Move the curve object to a different location, and press the **S** key to keyframe its new transformation values. Play the animation to see how the curve is moving from one side to another side, at the same time morphing from one shape to another shape.

5. Use **Create Animation Snapshot** with **Increment** set to 2. Click the **Apply** button and generate 120 curves. **Loft** these curves to a surface.

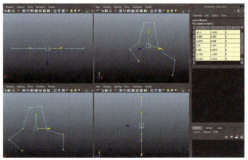

7.3.3 Step 2

7.3.3 Step 3

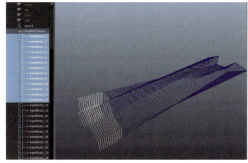

7.3.3 Step 4

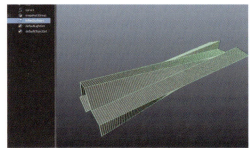

7.3.3 Step 5

8 DIGITAL FABRICATION

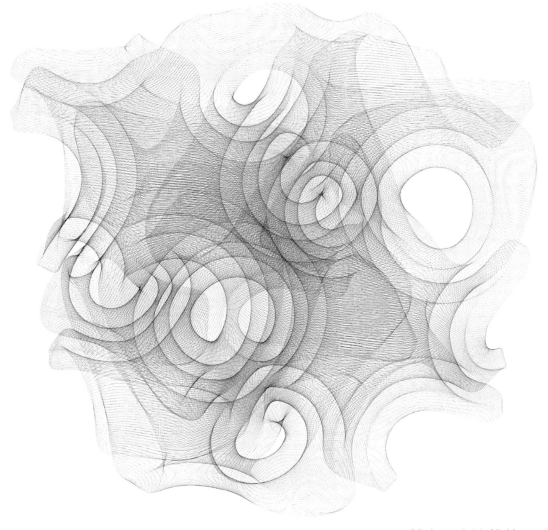

Mathmorph. MadCubic

8.1 CAD & CAM

Computer-aided design (CAD) and computer-aided manufacturing (CAM) have demonstrated a form of modeling that is sure to be widely adopted by the building industry. A computer can be used to design and fabricate components that form a building system. There are many applications of fabrication in architectural design, from early explorations using laser cutting and computer numerically controlled (CNC) milling processes in the mass customization, to the latest robotic manufacturing and large scale 3D printing.

Parametric thinking and CAM tools have yielded a significant innovation for designers to explore digital fabrication and material processing techniques. Laser cutting, CNC milling, and 3-D printing are available to designers as tools to assist in constructing complex digital models, and CAD technology has been developed extensively in the past two decades. Today, architects use various algorithms, scripts, and simulations to generate complex forms that move beyond conventional modeling techniques. Powerful digital tools allow designers to directly manipulate models without considering the constraints of the actual construction process.[1] There is a big difference between designing a building according to the geometry manipulation potential of software programs and the tectonic parameters of actual building materials. The distinction and relation between developing digital model and the fabrication process has been essential in parametric design.

Demonstrating the design process through Maya, this chapter focuses on techniques where information is not only just represented, but also processed through various pipelines to materialize the design. These techniques are described according to their relationship to laser cutting, CNC milling, and 3-D printing in a digital fabrication process that uses information to build the physical model. These techniques are introduced as a series of projects focusing making of physical product through mock-up models and material experiments. Digital representation (immaterial process) and fabrication (materialization process) are considered hybrid activities where designers engage in a nonlinear design pipeline. Digitally generated curvilinear forms lend themselves to fused deposition modeling (FDM), CNC milling, or laser cutting fabrication pipelines.

By Ari Pescovitz

DIGITAL FABRICATION

8.2. LASER CUTTING

8.2.1 Laser cutting 2-D patterns

Laser cutting has been widely used in building-product fabrication, such as the paneling system on the building façade. Maya provides a series of polygon-editing tools to generate patterns, including Extrude, Chamfer, Poke Face, and others. Designers can manipulate lines, points, and faces to create polygonal patterns. Deformations can also be applied to create organic tessellations, and models can be exported to other programs for further manipulation.[2]

Maya morphing and blending techniques covered in Chapter 3 can be used to create a series of overlaid panels that can be fabricated by laser cutting. Designers can create multiple layers and overlay panels to create rich visual effects. For instance, a polygon hexagonal shape can be used and morphed to various snowflakes. The panels can be assembled along several sliding tracks to control the sunlight and view. The overlays of these panels can be used to create an interesting heterogeneous composition.

Designers can also use a 3-D polygon surface to generate 2-D patterns. Faces on a 3-D surface can be selected manually based on their height and converted into different patterns, then the 3-D surface is flattened to produce a 2-D pattern for laser cutting.

Because the 2-D patterns are embedded in the polygon model, designers need to extract the wireframe cutting paths from the model and prepare the wireframe file for laser cutter.

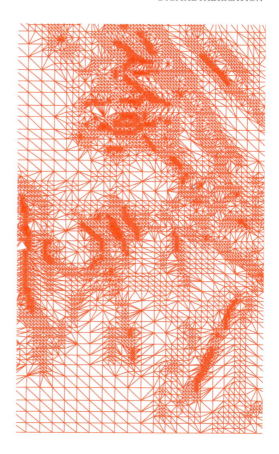

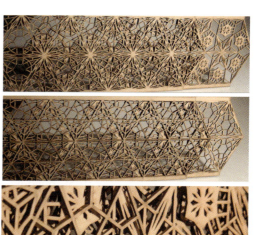

By Suncica Milosevic

151

DIGITAL FABRICATION

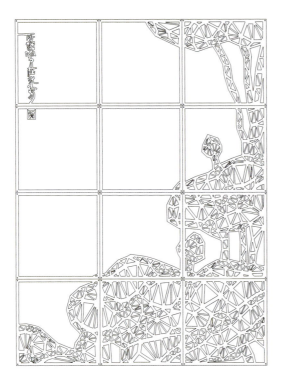

8.2.2 Files for laser cutting

There are several methods of generating a wireframe file from Maya polygon models. The goal of the operation is to create patterns and then translate the outlines into laser cutting paths. One method is to apply section cut in Rhino. A Maya polygon model can be first transformed into 3-D frames with Super Extrude MEL scripts and then exported to Rhino, where designers can cut a section to get wireframe cutting patterns.

Another method is to render the Maya model as a vector image.[3] The Maya vector renderer allows designers to generate vector format files that can be fed into a laser cutter. However, the vector rendering method may generate redundant lines or overlapping points, which need to be eliminated to avoid problems for laser cutting.

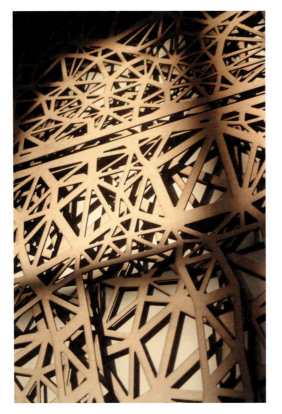

Water-lily. Tang & Yang Architects. The design started with a mesh pattern by converting a traditional Chinese painting into a polygon in Maya and then exporting it to Rhino. The Rhino section tool was used to generate the wireframe cutting pattern. Four foot by four foot masonite panels were fabricated to represent the original painting. Maya's Texture to Polygon tool can process a bitmap and create interesting tessellations within the polygon model.

DIGITAL FABRICATION

8.2.3 Laser cutting for 3-D objects

There are various laser-cutting methods to produce a physical model. Some can produce solid models to represent volumetric objects, while some can produce skin-like surface models.

Volumetric object

Maya can create objects with an enclosed surface and volume, such as a sphere, box, or cylinder. Objects like these can be fabricated by stacking a sequence of contoured slices. To extract contour wireframes from a 3-D model, designers can use a sequence of cutting planes to create series of contours. This process can be done by projecting curves onto an object in Maya, or using the Contour command to generate contour lines in Rhino. The thickness of the material should be considered so that the laser cut slices can add up to an accurate height and match with the digital model.

Another fabrication technique is to use waffle to represent a mass.[4] Similar as the contour technique, waffle is applied to two perpendicular axes to calculate the intersecting notches.

MathMorph. MadCubic. Model fabricated by stacking contoured slices.

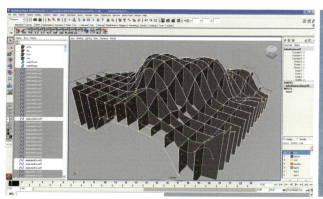

Waffle fabrication technique.

153

DIGITAL FABRICATION

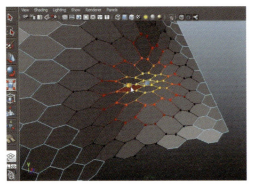

Surface model in Rhino.

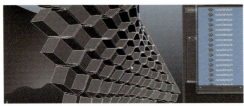

Soft manipulation in Maya.

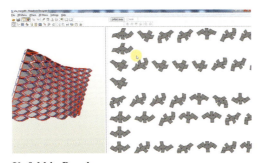

Extrude model in Maya.

Surface object

Maya can create nonvolumetric objects such as a surface to represent a curved wall. To use laser cutting to produce a curved surface, the surface needs to be tessellated into flat panels or broken into components that can be unrolled to flat shapes.[5] For instance, a curved beehive wall can be assembled with a large number of flat hexagonal planes or tapered hexagonal tubes that can be unfolded into 2-D shapes.

Models can be transferred across Maya and Rhino to take advantage of both programs. Designers can create a curved polygon surface in Maya with nCloth simulation and break the surface into flat panels. The surface can be exported to Rhino and manipulated to create flat panels in diamonds, hexagons, or other shapes. Then these panels are transferred back to Maya and modified by soft manipulation, extruded to individual boxes with certain depth. The model is exported to Rhino again to unroll or to third party software to unfold.[6]

Unfold in Pepakura.

By Natalie Levinson

DIGITAL FABRICATION

8.3 CNC

The CNC technique can be applied in both 2-D and 3-D fabrication. Milling a 2-D pattern is not different from laser cutting. The CNC tool head will follow the cutting paths and can mill various materials such as steel and plastic. It is also capable of moving along a complex 3-D path when operated with multiple axes.

8.3.1 Tool path

The movement of the cutting tool is called the *tool path*, which can be generated within CAM software such as Rhino CAM and Master CAM. CAM software can automatically create tool paths based on imported 3-D models and configurations of drill bits. For instance, a topography model can be milled by moving along multiple contour lines with different Z values. Advanced CAM programs also allow designers to convert curves directly into CNC paths. Designers can engrave a logo on a 3-D surface by using the logo outline curves to control the movement of the tool head. Maya can project curves on top of NURBS surfaces and produce various patterns like CNC tool paths. Depending on the shape of the drill bit, the milling process can create complex crafting results by leaving marks on the physical model.

For instance, designers can create a series of curves to form a 2-D pattern in Maya. The curves can be projected onto a 3-D surface in Maya and exported to CAM programs as tool paths. During the milling process, the drill bit follows the tool paths with a designated cutting depth and engraves the pattern onto the surface of the base material.

As an expensive fabrication technique, CNC is typically used to mill a mold and to cast into different materials such as resin or plastic. Mold casting and vacuum forming are efficient ways to mass produce identical parts for assembling a bigger system.[7]

Panels cut by CNC milling machine.

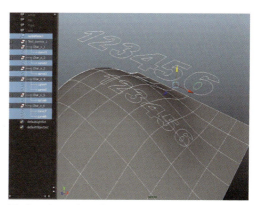

Tool path projected on the surface.

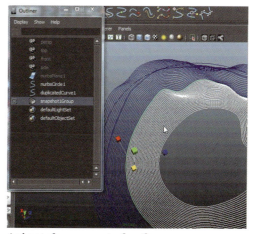

Animated curves as tool paths.

155

DIGITAL FABRICATION

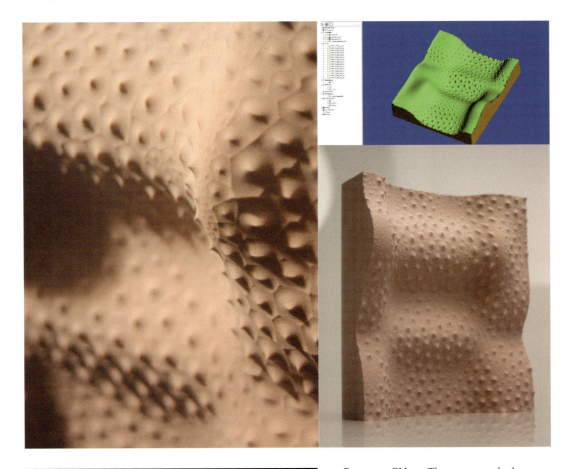

Dragon Skin. The engraved hexagon pattern was produced by creating curves in a mathematical pattern in Maya based on surface curvature. The curves were converted as tool paths in Master CAM and milled in a high density foam mold by CNC.

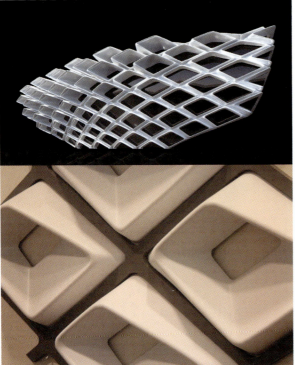

Scuta: Vacuum molding paneling system, by Andrew Newman. The original 3-D model was created in Maya, with several iterations controlled by the morphing technique. The panel mold was milled with CNC and used for vacuum molding to create the plastic panel. By Andrew Newman.

DIGITAL FABRICATION

8.4 3-D PRINT

3-D print is an additive manufacturing process done by adding layers of materials to make 3-D objects. This fabrication process can be categorized into two distinct applications: physical representation and physical prototyping. In physical representation, the digital fabrication is used as a communication tool, a physical representation medium, rather than a simulated construction process driven by tectonic principles. For instance, the end product of physical representation is a scaled 3-D building printed by a 3-D printer.

Physical prototyping simulates the construction process and considers all economic factors associated with the act of making. In simulating the manufacturing processes, the tool path, cutting time, and material property have to be carefully studied. The material and tectonic driven design process, 3-D printing a mold for casting spider joint, or 3-D printing building panels with cement all belong to the physical prototyping. The difference between prototyping and representation is that prototyping is typically used to test materials or joints, assembled in full scale to demonstrate manufacturing and construction procedures. While physical representation produces small-scale models to present the design for communication purposes.

When using a surface modeling program like Maya, only objects with closed surfaces can be 3-D printed. The closed surface model must be read as a volumetric model in 3-D printing. In Maya, there are various tools to convert an open surface model to a closed surface model. For instance, the Extrude tool can take an open surface model to create volumetric solid shells.

Some modeling issues will make geometry invalid for 3-D printing. These issues include missing faces, self-intersecting faces, naked edges, overlapping vertices, reversed normal, and others.[8] Designers can use the Maya Clean Up tool to fix these issues and create a seamless closed-surface model. Some 3-D print programs can automatically check the normal directions and fix the holes.

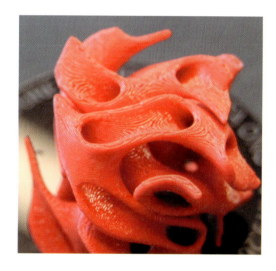

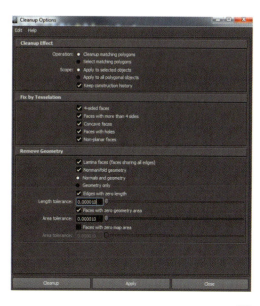

157

DIGITAL FABRICATION

8.5 CASE STUDY

8.5.1 Mathmorph

Mathmorph is a series of abstract sculptures designed to experiment with 3-D printing and the laser-cutting process. The goal was to use Maya to manipulate mathematically generated models, add complexity, and prepare files for fabrication. Designers added a sequence of Maya operations to control the math model parametrically, including the thickness of the shell, the size of voids, and the angles of interlocking. These parameters allowed unlimited possibilities in the configuration between solid forms and void spaces. Designers also adapted several parameters to control the repetition, resolution,

Mathmorph. MadCubic.

and deformation of the math forms. Maya Clean Up tools were used to yield a more 3-D-printing-friendly form. Maya projection and Rhino section tools were used to extract wireframe curves for laser cutting. As the result, designers created a high degree of complexity and explored the possibilities of fabrication with 3-D printing and laser cutting. In both processes, Maya demonstrated its great power and potential for manipulating and preparing forms for fabrication.

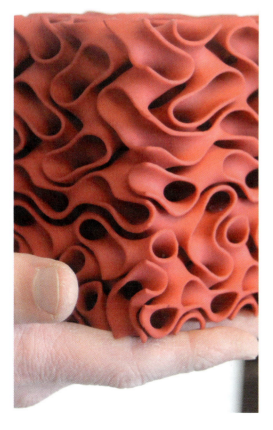

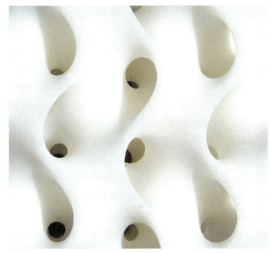

DIGITAL FABRICATION

Fractal Panel. MadCubic. (Photography by Jonathon Anderson).

8.5.2 Fractal imprint

The *fractal imprint* project explored the process of using Maya to manipulate 2-D mathematic patterns and generate corresponding 3-D forms for CNC milling. First, the complexity and resolution of the NURBS surface were controlled mathematically by a 2-D fractal pattern image. The 2-D image was generated using mathematic equations and translated into 3-D displacement map in Maya. [9] Pixel values of the 2-D image controlled the depressions and elevations, which were used to sculpt the surface.

Designers selected the desired control parameters to manipulate the displacement map, which represented the mathematic fractal pattern and generated spatial organization. The 3-D model was deciphered into a readable CNC data file to mill the mold, which was then used to produce plastic panels with the vacuum-forming technique.

8.6 FUTURE OF CAD AND CAM

Over the past several years, designers have explored the ways to integrate CAD and CAM tools into the parametrically controlled design process. By exploring innovative methods to use the available fabrication technologies, designers inevitably improve design processes and integrate digital fabrication into the design pipeline. Experimentations with advanced parametric programs like Maya can yield new techniques for design and build. Digital fabrication has given architects the tools needed to transform conceptual ideas into built environments with artifacts that were deemed unbuildable virtual objects.

8.7 TUTORIAL: TOOL PATH MAKING

1. Create a NURBS surface and a circle in the top view.

2. Select both objects and use **Project Curve on Surface** in the **Edit NURBS** menu to project the circle onto the surface.

3. Move the original circle to observe how the projected curve on the surface is moving along with the circle.

4. Hold the right mouse button on top of the NURBS surface and choose **Isoparm** as the component selection. Then select the projected circle on the surface.

5. Use **Duplicate Surface Curves** from the **Edit Curves** menu to create a new curve based on the selection. The new curve is visible in the **Outliner** window. When moving the original circle, the duplicated one will follow. Rename the duplicated curve as *duplicatedcurve*. The curve will be exported later to the milling program as a tool path.

6. When multiple tool paths are desired, animate the original circle and use **animation snapshot** technique to create multiple projects on the surface as following steps:

7. Modify the timeline to 100 frames. Move to frame 1 and select the original circle, press the **S** key in the keyboard to record the current transformation attributes. These channels on the right side of the screen should turn to red color.

8. Move the timeline to frame 100 and scale up the original circle. Press the **S** key to record the new attribute values. Play the animation.

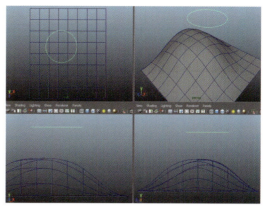

8.7 Step 1

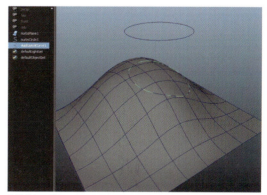

8.7 Step 3

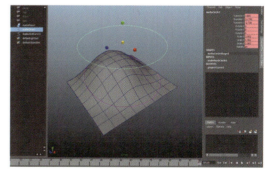

8.7 Step 7

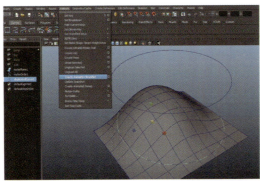

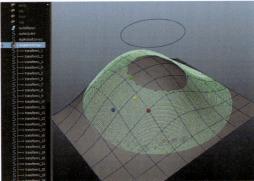

8.7 Step 9

9. Because Maya remembers all the relationship among objects and nodes, the animated circle will drive the projected curve and the duplicated curve. Select the *duplicatedcurve* in the **Outliner** window. Use the **Create Animation Snapshot** tool in the **Animate** menu to create duplications along the timeline. Set the **Increment** value to 2, which will generate 50 curves along the timeline.

10. Export the 50 curves as an IGES file and load it into a CNC milling program such as PowerMill as the tool path file.

9 SCRIPTING

Scripting language is written for a software, Web page, or operating system to automatically execute tasks. The widespread scripting languages include Javascript, PHP, and Perl. The Maya program embeds both Phython and Maya Embedded Language (MEL) scripts. Phython script is also used in many other programs besides Maya, such as Houdini and Nuke, while MEL was developed in the early version of Maya and only operates in the Maya environment. MEL script is easier to learn for non-programmers than the Phython script is. This chapter focuses on how to write a simple MEL script by observing the logged commands in the script window, constructing MEL script with correct syntax, and writing a particular user interface for inputting variables.[1]

9.1 MEL SCRIPT

MEL is a specific scripting language developed for Maya operation. The graphic designer interface (GUI) of Maya was built based on MEL script, which remains largely unchanged since the early versions of Maya software. MEL script can directly manipulate nodes, connections, and attributes. It offers a method to manage complicated tasks and speed up repetitive operations. Designers can subdivide complicated operation into multiple smaller and more manageable operations in MEL script. The script can recall these suboperation procedures in the master script to handle complicated operations.

Among the various methods of learning MEL scripting, the easiest way is looking at the command log window after a specific operation is completed. For example, designers can create a polygon sphere through menus and tool bars. As soon as the sphere is created, the command log in the Script Editor window will automatically post the MEL script that has just been executed. Designers will see the script as following:

setToolTo CreatePolySphereCtx;
polySphere -ch on -o on -r 2.006133;

This is the actual script with which MEL generates the sphere. Designers can copy and paste these two lines of script at the bottom of the MEL script editor window under the MEL tag, highlight all the pasted script and use **Control + Enter** or **Execute** button in the script editor window to execute the script. Maya will generate the same result instantly.

The second line can also be changed with a new radius value as the following:

polySphere -ch on -o on -r 10;

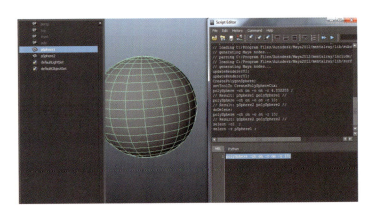

By executing the above script, a polygon sphere will be generated with the radius of 10. To get more details about the polySphere script in MEL, designers can use the MEL script reference from the Help menu or Autodesk Maya Help website to find more information. [2] In these sources, designers can also find long name (short name) flags such as –radius (-r), -subdivisionsX (-sx), -subdivisionsY (-sy), and so on.

Now designers can rewrite the script as:

polySphere -ch on -o on -r 10 -sx 5
-sy 5;

This time, executing the above script will result in a new polygon sphere with the radius of 10 and a 5 by 5 subdivision. Designers can also execute multiple actions. For instance, if the designer first moved the sphere along Y axis 13 units, and then rotated it along Z axis 90 degrees, the command log in the upper window of the script editor window will automatically show the following:

move -r 0 13 0;
rotate -r -ws 0 0 90;

It is easy to figure out that the three values shown after *–r* flag are X, Y, and Z values. Designers can add a new value and compose a three-line script:

polySphere -ch on -o on -r 10 -sx 5
-sy 5;
move -r 0 8 0;
rotate -r -ws 0 0 -90;

When a designer executes the above script, Maya will generate a sphere, move it, and rotate it based on the input values of X, Y, and Z, which will be recorded in the Transformation channel of pSphere1.

A MEL script can be saved as a MEL file,

independent from any specific Maya scene file, for reloading in other Maya scene files or editing in word processing software. When reloading a MEL file, designers can select the file and hold the middle mouse button to drag it into the shelf to create a shortcut, which can be renamed in the Shelf Editor window.[3] When clicking the shortcut, Maya will execute the MEL script to complete the operation it specified. Such MEL script is highly efficient for performing repetitive operations.

SCRIPTING

9.2 TUTORIALS

9.2.1 Tutorial: Super Extrude

This tutorial demonstrates how to compose a Super Extrude MEL script that includes a sequence of commands to create a polygon frame based on the existing polygon tessellations. The goal is to convert every edge of an existing polygon model into a 3-D frame. Designers can use polygon-editing tools to modify the tessellation of the polygon model before applying the MEL script. After applying the MEL script, the standard Smooth tool can be used to convert the faceted model into a bone-like structure. Because Maya records all the actions and values in the history INPUTS node, designers can easily access the actions generated by the MEL script, revise the parameters, and observe the new outcomes in a nonlinear design process.[4]

The MEL script for executing the Super Extrude operation has three parts. The first part is to select all the faces of the object. Second, create a window and input fields to input values, which will be read as input variables by the operation. Last, use the values entered in the input fields to initiate a series of actions to create

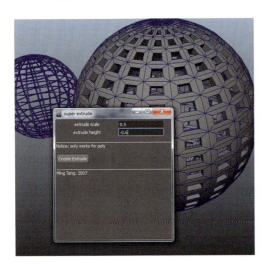

frames. Among these steps, the second step consists of a series of sequential actions including using all the faces of the object to create individual extruded faces, scaling down these new faces to create an offset effect, deleting the offset faces to create openings, and extruding the entire mesh by a thickness value entered in the input field created in the second action.

//This script will use a polygon model (mesh) to generate lattice frames. A polygon model is required. Select it first and run the script.

Any text following the two virgules, **//**, are notes and will be ignored in the execution. It is a good practice to write notes to explain the function of the following script for future reference or easy understanding by other programmers.

//Select faces.

Get ready to select all the faces from a polygon model and add certain operations to them.

proc extrudepoly()
{

A procedure named **extrudepoly** is created. This procedure's name will be called from the user interface when clicking the specific button, so it is important to give it a unique name. The braces, **{}**, define the beginning and the end of the procedure.

float $escale = `textField -q -text escale`;

The dollar sign, **$**, defines a variable called **escale**. Its type is a floating point. The value is extracted from the user input window, a text field called *escale*.

float $edist = `textField -q -text edist`;

166

Another variable named ***edist*** is defined. The value is extracted from the user input window, a text field named *edist*.

string $myobject[] = `ls -sl`;

Create a new variable named ***myobject***. Its type is a string, and is used to host the currently selected object's name; **–sl** stands for selection.

print ("the query name is" + $myobject[0]);

The print command provides a good check point for debugging. If there is anything wrong with the *myobject* variable, Maya will display an error message.

$item = $myobject[0] + ".f[0:99999]";

Create a variable named ***item***. Then use **f.[ ]** to select all the faces of the polygon model. The number **99999** is set to define the maximum face amount of the polygon model, which can be changed if necessary.

select -cl;

Clean the current selection because all the faces are already saved into the variable named ***item***.

select -r $item;

Select all the faces saved in the ***item*** variable.

//Extrude by scale.
//Select -r $myobject[0].f[0:9999];
polyExtrudeFacet -ch 1 -kft 0 -lsx $escale -lsy $escale -lsz $escale;

Use **polyExtrudeFacet** script to extrude every face.

Flag **–ch 1**: Construction History is on.

Flag **–kft 0**: Keep Face Together is off.

Flag **–lsx**: Local scale X, with the value defined by variable ***escale*** typed in the user input window.

Flag **–lsy**: Local scale Y, with the value defined by variable ***escale***.

Flag **–lsz**: Local scale Z, with the value defined by variable ***escale***.

As the result, all the new extruded faces are scaled down based on a user defined value, which creates the offset effect.

doDelete;

Delete all the newly extruded faces, resulting in an opening on every face.

//Extrude again.
select -r $item;

Select all the faces again. Since all the new generated faces are deleted, what are left are the original faces.

polyExtrudeFacet -ch 1 -kft 1 -ltz $edist;

Extrude all the faces again.

Flag **–kft 1**: Keep Face Together is on. All faces will be extruded as a group.

Flag **–ltz**: Local translate Z value, with the value defined by variable ***edist*** typed in the user input window.

This second extrusion creates the depth for the frame.

}

A brace, **}**, defines the end of the procedure.

//Create a user interface (UI) window.

Create a user interface window to collect variables for the **extrudpoly** procedural.

global proc extrudewin ()

Because designers need to call the variables from outside, this **extrudewin** procedure needs to be set as global so its variables are accessible from the **extrudepoly** procedure.

{
if (`window -exists extrudeWindow`) {
deleteUI extrudeWindow; }

This script checks whether the same window has been created before. If so, delete the existing window.

window
-widthHeight 300 300
-title "super extrude"
-sizeable true
extrudeWindow;

Create a new window. Name it **extrudeWindow**.

//Add two values.

columnLayout;
rowColumnLayout -numberOfColumns 2
-columnWidth 1 120
-columnSpacing 1 20
-columnWidth 2 120
-columnSpacing 2 20;

Create two columns with specific width and spacing.

text -l "extrude scale";
textField -tx 0.9 escale ;
text -l "extrude height";
textField -tx -0.1 edist ;
setParent ..;

Add two text labels and two text fields. The first text field is to collect values for variable **escale**, the second is to collect values for variable **edist**. These variables will be read by the **extrudepoly** procedural later. **SetParent** ends the two column layout.

//break
text -l "";
separator -w 800;

The separator provides a dividing line to help create a clear layout.

text -l "Notice: only works for poly";
text -l "";

//three buttons
rowColumnLayout -numberOfColumns 1;

Create a new column layout with one column.

//Create button 1.
button -label "Create Extrude"
-command "extrudepoly" extrudepoly;

Create a button named **Create Extrude**, which triggers the **extrudepoly** procedure.

setParent ..;

End the column layout.

//break
columnLayout;
text -l "";
separator -w 800;
text -l "Ming Tang. 2014";

Set a new column layout and add texts.

showWindow;

This script displays the window once it is completed.

}

A brace, **}**, closes the **extrudewin** procedure.

extrudewin;

The last line of the script executes the **extrudewin** procedural.

9.2.2 Tutorial: Random weave

This tutorial starts from the Super Extrude script made in the previous tutorial and adds several random cuts to create a weaving effect similar to the structure system used in the Beijing National Stadium. Most of the script is identical to the Super Extrude script.

//This script will use a polygon model (mesh surface) to generate the weave pattern.
//A polygon model is required.
//Select it first and run the script.
//Cut face to create weave pattern.

proc extrudepoly()
{
int $ncut = `textField -q -text ncut`;
float $escale = `textField -q -text escale`;
float $edist = `textField -q -text edist`;
string $myobject[] = `ls -sl`;
print ("the quary name is" + $myobject[0]);

//Create weave pattern.
//string $myobject[] = `ls -sl`;
//Print ("the quary name is" + $myobject[0]);

float $bound[]=
`exactWorldBoundingBox $myobject`;

In order to cut the polygon model correctly, it is necessary to collect its bounding box value to set the cutting range. **ExactWordBoundingBox** generates six values based on the minimum and maximum X, Y, Z values and assigns them to a new variable named **bound**.

for($n = 0; $n < $ncut; $n++)

The following looping operation will be repeated several times. The counter is initially assigned as 0 and will increase 1 each time until it reaches the number **ncut**.

{

A brace, **{**, defines the start point a loop.

$xx=rand($bound[0], $bound[3]);
$yy=rand($bound[1], $bound[4]);
$zz=rand($bound[2], $bound[5]);

Create three random numbers within the bounding box based on its width, depth, and height. A random point can be created within the bounding box.

$rxx=rand(-180, 180);
$ryy=rand(-180, 180);
$rzz=rand(-180, 180);

Create three random numbers for cutting angles along X, Y, and Z axes.

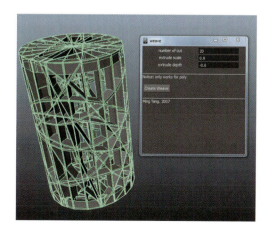

SCRIPTING

```
polyCut -ch on -pc $xx $yy $zz -ro
$rxx $ryy $rzz $myobject;
```

Flag **–ch**: Construction History is on.

Flag **–pc**: Define the position of a cutting plane by a random point in the bounding box.

Flag **–ro**: Define the random orientation of the cutting plane.

$myobject is the target object of the Polygon Cut action.

```
}
```

A brace, **}**, defines the closing point of a loop.

 The rest of the script is identical to the Super Extrude script.

```
//Create polyextrude.

$item = $myobject[0] + ".f[0:99999]";
select -cl;

//Poker face to add details. It is a
better way than triangulating.
//PolyPoke -ws 1 -tx 0 -ty 0 -tz 0 -ltx 0
-lty 0 -ltz 0 -ch 1 $myobject[0];

select -r $item;

//Extrude by scale.
//Select -r $myobject[0].f[0:9999];
polyExtrudeFacet -ch 1 -kft 0 -lsx
$escale -lsy $escale -lsz $escale;
doDelete;

//Extrude again.

select -r $item ;
polyExtrudeFacet -ch 1 -kft 1 -ltz
$edist;
}
```

```
//Create UI window.

global proc extrudewin ()
{
if (`window -exists extrudeWindow`) {
deleteUI extrudeWindow; }
window
-widthHeight 300 300
-title "weave"
-sizeable true
extrudeWindow;

//Add three values.
columnLayout;
rowColumnLayout
-numberOfColumns 2
-columnWidth 1 120
-columnSpacing 1 20
-columnWidth 2 120
-columnSpacing 2 20;

text -l "number of cut";
textField -tx 20 ncut ;
```

Define the text field for the designer to input values for a variable named **ncut**, which is called from **extrudepoly** to control the times of operating the **polyCut** action.

```
text -l "extrude scale";
textField -tx 0.9 escale ;
text -l "extrude depth";
textField -tx -0.1 edist ;
setParent ..;

//break
text -l "";
separator -w 800;
text -l "Notice: only works for poly";
text -l "";

//three buttons
rowColumnLayout
-numberOfColumns 1;

//Create button 1.
```

```
button -label "Create Weave"
-command "extrudepoly" extrudepoly;
setParent ..;

//break
columnLayout;
text -l "";
separator -w 800;
text -l "Ming Tang. 2007";
showWindow;
}

extrudewin;
```

9.2.3 Tutorial: Image sampling

Image sampling is a process to extract RGB and alpha values from an image and use them to drive operations parametrically. This tutorial demonstrates an example of using image sampling to generate a pattern with circular perforation for laser cutting.

```
//Populate a surface with 2D shapes
controlled by an image.
//Use a TIFF image to control the
geometry populated on the XZ plane.
//The RGB and alpha values are
extracted from the TIFF image and
are used to drive the scale.
//One object needs to be created with
1 by 1 bounding box, and named as
shape01. It will be populated across a
rectangular surface.

{
//Load an external image and sample
its RGB and alpha values.
//image mapping
string $filenode = `createNode file`;
```

Create a file node.

```
string $shader = `createNode
lambert`;
```

Create a lambert shader.

```
//This is the path to the external TIFF
file. Make sure to have the alpha
channel in the TIFF file.
string $path = "C:/TM/topo-house17.
TIF";
```

Create the path to an image file. Update the path to the local folder. The TIFF file needs to include RGB and alpha Channels.

```
//Connect the nodes.
connectAttr ($filenode + ".outColor")
($shader + ".color");
```

Connect the image file node to Maya lambert shader's color channel.

```
//Insert the image path in the file
node.
string $map = $path;
setAttr -type "string" ($filenode +
".fileTextureName") $map;
```

Connect the image file as the texture path. Now the TIFF image is connected to the lambert shader.

```
string $object[] = `nurbsPlane -ax 0 1
0 -w 100 -lr 1 -name "nurbsPlane1"`;
```

Create a new NURBS plane with 100 units.

SCRIPTING

```
//Assign the shader to an object.
select -r $object[0];
hyperShade -assign $shader;
```

Assign the lambert shader to the NURBS plane.

```
int $u, $v,
$nu = 50, $nv = 50; // steps in u and v
```

Define the sampling divisions along U and V.

```
float $minU = 0, $minV = 0, // u/v -
start and ending
$maxU = 1, $maxV = 1; // the surface
- slightly less than 0 to 1
```

```
//Grab all our texture map samples.
float $rgb[] = `colorAtPoint -o RGBA
-su $nu -sv $nv -mu $minU -mv
$minV
-xu $maxU -xv $maxV $filenode`;
```

Check the color value based on the samplesU (50) and samplesV (50) within the sample bounds (0-1). As the result, the **rgb[ ]** array contains four values (RGB+alpha) for each point.

```
float $deltaU = ($maxU - $minU)/($nu
- 1); // step size in u
float $deltaV = ($maxV - $minV)/($nv
- 1); // step size in v
```

Define the increment for sampling.

```
float $currU, $currV;
int $index = 0;
$currU = $minU;
```

Set the initial U value to start the loop.

```
for($n = 0; $n < $nu; $n++)
{
$currU += $deltaU;
```

Set U increment for sampling.

```
$currV = $minV;
```

Set the initial V value to start the loop.

```
for($i = 0; $i < $nv; $i++)
```

The **for( )** loop can be used to extract the RGB and alpha values from every UV point.

```
{
float $r = $rgb[$index];
float $g = $rgb[$index + 1];
float $b = $rgb[$index + 2];
float $a = $rgb[$index + 3];
print($r + " " + $g + " " + $b + " " + $a
+ "\n");
```

Because every UV point contains RGB and alpha values, designers need to extract these four values one by one from the array.

```
if( ($r + $g + $b) < 3)
```

RGB and alpha values are between 0 to 1. Their values can be modified to filter out some points if necessary.

```
{
float $p[] = `pointOnSurface
-u $currU
-v $currV
$object[0]`;
```

Locate a specific point based on its U and V values. X Y Z values are saved in the list P.

```
string $listA[]={"shape01"};
```

Load the **shape01** object for future operations.

```
//Create a scaled duplication based
on RGB and Alpha values.
```

SCRIPTING

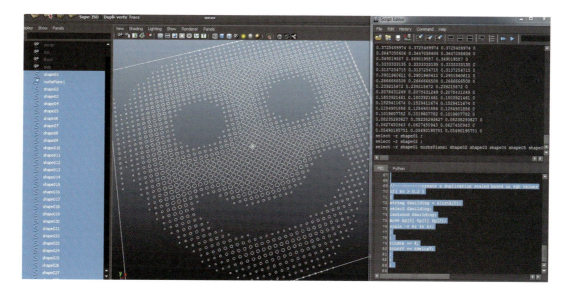

if($r > 0.2)

Only UV points with red color value greater than 0.2 will be applied with the following operations.

{
string $building = $listA[0];
select $building;
instance $building;
move $p[0] $p[1] $p[2];

Copy the object and move it to a specific UV point. X Y Z values of the UV point are extracted from list P.

scale -r $r $r $r;

Scale the object based on the red color value.

}
}
$index += 4;

Because every point contains four values (RGB and alpha values), so the loop will be stepped with interval value 4.

$currV += $deltaV;

Update current V with the increment and start the loop again.

}
}
}

9.2.4 Tutorial: Zoning map for a digital city

Designers can sample the RGB and alpha values from an image and use them to drive the 3-D modeling. In this tutorial, the color red generates commercial buildings, green generates residential buildings, and alpha channel defines building orientation. The form of each commercial building is randomly selected from three prototypes named *building01*, *building02,* and *building03*, while the form of each residential building is selected from prototypes *building04*, *building05*, and *building06*. Designers can also use different colors in an image map to control the populating of various buildings to create an urban model. For instance, a geographic information system (GIS) map can be used to generate demographic and social layers based on

173

US Census Data; therefore the designers can visualize this nongeometric data with 3-D urban forms.

//Use a TIFF image to control the geometry populated on the XZ plane.
//The RGB and alpha channels are extracted from the TIFF image and used to drive other operations such as move, rotate, or scale.
//Six objects need to be created and named as building01, building02, building03, building04, building05, and building06.
//Ming Tang. 2013. http:///ming3d.com

{
//Load an external image and sample its RGB and alpha values.
//image mapping
string $filenode = `createNode file`;
string $shader = `createNode lambert`;
string $path = "C:/TM/topo-house16.TIF";

The path should be modified according to the file name.

//Connect the nodes.
connectAttr ($filenode + ".outColor")

By Boer Deng

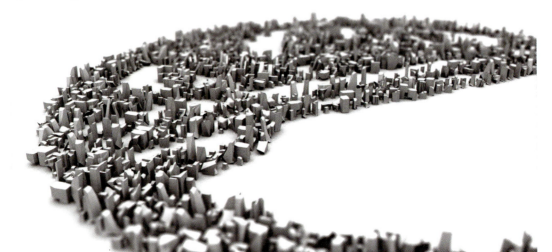

By Kate Bogenschutz

```
($shader + ".color");

//Insert the image path in the file
node.
string $map = $path;
setAttr -type "string" ($filenode +
".fileTextureName") $map;

string $object[] = `nurbsPlane -ax 0 1
0 -w 100 -lr 1 -name "nurbsPlane1"`;
select -r $object[0];
hyperShade -assign $shader;
int $u, $v,
$nu = 50, $nv = 50; // steps in u and v
float $minU = 0, $minV = 0, // u/v -
start and ending
$maxU = 1, $maxV = 1;

//Collect texture map samples.
float $rgb[] = `colorAtPoint -o RGBA
-su $nu -sv $nv -mu $minU -mv
$minV
-xu $maxU -xv $maxV $filenode`;
float $deltaU = ($maxU - $minU)/($nu
- 1); // step size in u
float $deltaV = ($maxV - $minV)/($nv
- 1); // step size in v

float $currU, $currV;
int $index = 0;
$currU = $minU;
for($n = 0; $n < $nu; $n++)
{
$currU += $deltaU;
$currV = $minV;
for($i = 0; $i < $nv; $i++)
{
float $r = $rgb[$index];
float $g = $rgb[$index + 1];
float $b = $rgb[$index + 2];
float $a = $rgb[$index + 3];
print($r + " " + $g + " " + $b + " " + $a
+ "\n");
if( ($r + $g + $b) < 2)
{
float $p[] = `pointOnSurface
-u $currU
-v $currV
$object[0]`;
string $listA[]={"building01",
"building02", "building03"};
string $listB[]={"building04",
"building05", "building06"};
string $listC[]={"building01",
"building02", "building03",
```

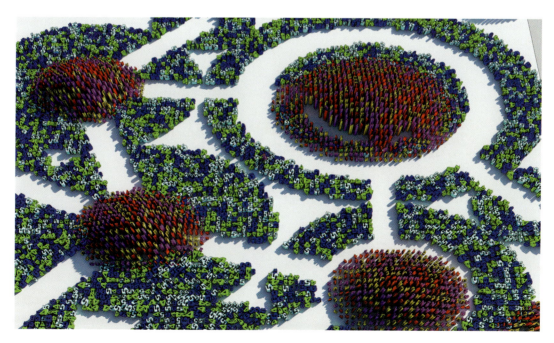

SCRIPTING

"building04", "building05", "building06"};

Group building types to several lists.

//Red color value controls commercial buildings.

Use red color to define areas to populate commercial buildings.

```
if( $r > 0.8 )
{
int $number = rand(0,3);
string $building = $listA[$number];
```

List A is the commercial building group which contains *building01*, *building02*, and *building03*.

```
select $building;
instance $building;
scale -r (rand(1, 2)) (rand(2, 4)) 1;
move $p[0] $p[1] $p[2];
rotate -r 0 ((-360)*$a) 0;
```

```
int $rottime = rand(0,4);
rotate -r 0 (90*$rottime) 0;
```

Rotate the building randomly by 0, 90, 180, and 270 degrees.

```
}
```

//Green color value controls residential buildings.

Use green color to define areas to populate residential buildings.

```
if($g > 0.8)
{
int $number = rand(0,3);
string $building = $listB[$number];
```

List B is the residential building group which contains *building04*, *building05*, and *building06*.

```
select $building;
instance $building;
```

scale -r (rand(1, 3)) (rand(1, 2)) (rand(1, 2));
move $p[0] $p[1] $p[2];
rotate -r 0 ((-360)$a) 0;*
int $rottime = rand(0,4);
*rotate -r 0 (90*$rottime) 0;*

Rotate the building randomly by 0, 90, 180, and 270 degrees.

}
}
$index += 4;
$currV += $deltaV;
}
}
}

This image sampling method can be used on a large urban scale as well. From a city planner's viewpoint, complex zoning codes can be represented by various colors on a map, such as red for commercial zones and blue for residential zones. In Maya, designers can extract these colors from a 2-D map representing the city, use colors to distribute the zoning rules, and thus construct a 3-D city model.

Using "colorAtPoint" MEL script, designers can extract the RGB and alpha values per vertex and trigger duplicate operations according to the predefined rules. This method can be called the *traffic light* approach, where the driver's action (pass/stop) is based on the color of the traffic lights (red, yellow, or green). The same logic can be applied to the image sampling method. For instance, if the color in a specific point is red (red channel value equals 1 in Maya), designers can instruct Maya to create a specific object in that point. Designers can also set mathematical thresholds to evaluate these RGB and alpha values with "if" and "or" conditions. This approach provides a method of linking colors with actions.

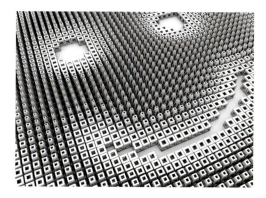

In this method, a raster image is produced in Photoshop by painting colors in the RGB and alpha channels. The color is saved on the pixel level and loaded into Maya by MEL script. There are two important differences in this image sampling approach compared to the vertex color approach discussed in the previous chapter. First, because all colors are operated on a pixel level instead of computed on vertex level, designers have greater flexibility to manipulate colors with image-editing programs such as Photoshop. Designers can apply filters or blend multiple images with layers. Second, the image sampling approach requires a projecting/mapping technique to control how colors are distributed across the 3-D surface, so designers have the flexibility to use all the Maya projection tools to control the relation between colors and geometries. Various projection types such as planar, cylindrical, or UV Wrap projection can also be chosen to control the result. It is difficult to achieve the same result through vertex color.

From these tutorials, the great benefit of using MEL to execute repetitive actions was explained. Now it is time to build your own MEL script. You can start with planning what the script will do and how you want it to work. Once you have a clear idea how to break down the design problem into the basic steps, you need to build and test the script.

SCRIPTING

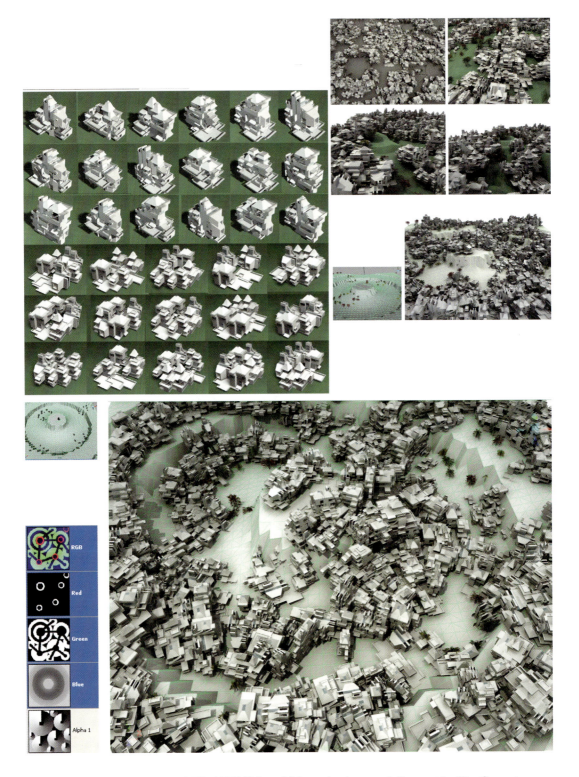

Parametric City Generator. An MEL / TCL11 based Maya plug-in named *Parametric City Generator*, was developed to integrate geographic information system (GIS) into parametric modeling techniques. This plug-in could automatically generate 3-D urban forms by interpreting 2-D GIS maps and database.

SCRIPTING

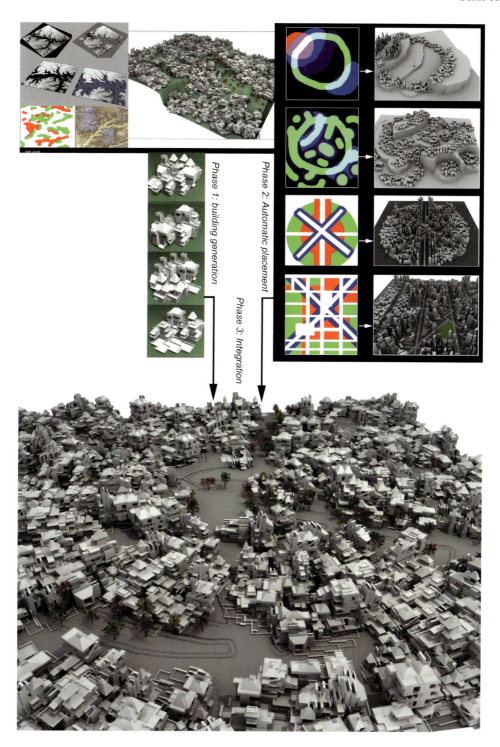

First, several basic building units were modeled and imported into *Parametric City Generator*. Then the designers executed the breeding process and produced a large number of offspring in the first generation. This process was finished by a combination of the original units' genotype. The second part of this project was using the selected housing units to grow the city according to GIS data. The goal was to simulate possible urban fabrics for a diagram city that grows from a natural context rather than an imposed gridiron pattern.

SCRIPTING

10 IN AND OUT

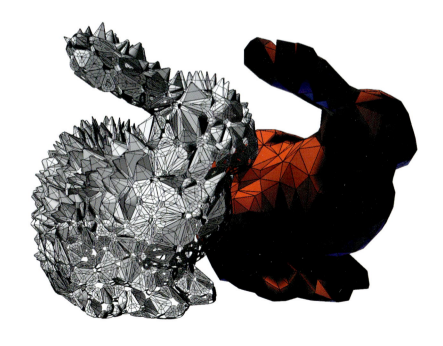

CAD software has been extensively developed since the early computer drafting programs of the 1980s. Some software allows designers to directly manipulate complex building information. Some are specially designed to analyze certain information, such as the building energy model and structural analysis. Today, the building modeling software in the architectural design field includes AutoCAD, ArchiCAD, Sketch up, Revit, 3D Studio Max, Blender, CATIA, Cinema 4D, Maya, Rhino, Form Z, Micro Station, Generative Component, and more.

10.1 TRANSFER DATA ACROSS PROGRAMS

All 3-D programs allow designers to create and modify models via manipulation tools. Most of them provide a number of common features such as material editing and rendering facilities. Some also contain features that support animation or physic simulation. Models can be exported to various types of universal file formats, which can then be imported into other programs.[1]

It is increasingly evident that the design information is often transferred across several programs in various design phases. A conceptual model might be initially created in Sketch up and later transferred to Rhino to create details. A building information model might be generated in Revit and transferred to 3dsMAX or Maya for advanced modeling and rendering operations. Therefore, it is important to understand how standard materials are constructed and what material properties can be transferred among various programs.

10.2 IMPORT DATA INTO MAYA

With import and export plug-ins, Maya is able to read and write data in various formats. Transferring geometries from other programs into Maya is straightforward. Designers can import models in 3DS, OBJ, DXF, DWG, FBX, IGES, and other formats directly into Maya. Among these file formats, Autodesk FBX format also allows designers to transfer camera, light, animation, and material into Maya in addition to the geometries. However, it is a good practice to make sure all imported materials are standard shaders so they can be read in Maya. There are several common components to formulate a standard shader material, no matter which 3-D program is used. These components include basic map channels, as well as a file path to a linked texture file. Designers should convert nonstandard materials into standard ones that can be understood by Maya. The relations between materials and associated geometries are preserved when the FBX file is imported into Maya.

10.3 EXPORT DATA FROM MAYA

Maya allows designers to export geometries through OBJ, DXF, FBX, IGES, and other file formats. The FBX format can support exporting Maya light, material, and animation into other programs. Designers can also embed the lighting and material information into the geometry as vertex color for exporting, as discussed in previous chapters. Lighting, material, and bitmap texture can be converted directly into vertex color. Depending on the point density and tessellation of the polygon model, the color value can be represented by color per vertex (CPV). This method allows easy transferring of data across multiple software programs. For example,

IN AND OUT

designers can export data from advanced shaders and projections by baking the result into vertex color. Because the vertex's CPV data and the geometry are exported together, their relations are preserved and can be used to control further operations in other programs. Designers can even paint vertex color with an artistic expression and later decode these prepainted colors as rules to modify the geometry in other programs.

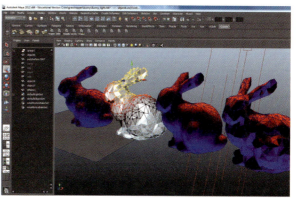
Maya

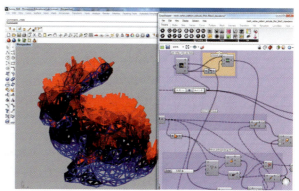
Rhino

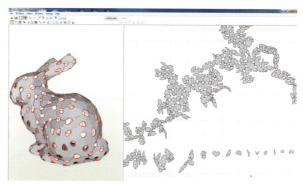
Pepakura

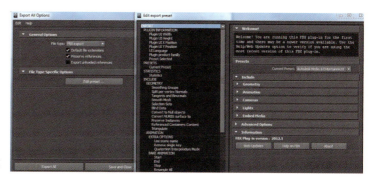
FBX Export Setting

183

IN AND OUT

Tessellations created in Rhino based on Maya vertex color.

10.4 TUTORIALS

10.4.1 Tutorial: From Revit to Maya

1. Create a curtain wall system with Revit materials.

2. **Export** the model from Revit as FBX format.

3. Launch 3dsMax. Use the **File > Reference > File Link Manger** tool to link the FBX file to the program. Click the **Attach** button.

4. Now the curtain wall should contain three colors. The designer can load the object's material in the **Material Editor** Window. The Revit material is brought in as a **Multi/Sub_**object material due to Revit family settings.

5. Click the **Material/Map Navigator** button to open the sub materials. Change each of them from Autodesk **Generic** material to **Standard** material.

6. **Export** the 3dsMax file to an FBX file.

7. Launch Maya program. **Import** the new FBX file. All the materials from 3dsMax are imported.

8. Double click the purple color shader in the **Hypershade** window in Maya to open its attribute panel. Assign a procedural texture named **Checker** to its **Color** channel.

9. Modify its **Transparency** channel.

10. Group all objects by the **Control + G** or **Edit > Group** tool. Use the **Modify > Center Pivot** tool to snap the center point automatically back to the volumetric center. Now these objects can be manipulated as one group.

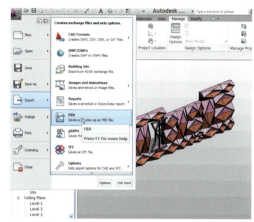
10.4.1 Step 2

10.4.1 Step 5

10.4.1 Step 8

11. Select the group node. Click the **Nonlinear Bend** tool in the **Deformation** shelf, or use the **Create Deformers > Nonlinear > Bend** tool in the **Animation** menu group. Rotate the bend handle to make it parallel to the curtain wall. Click the **Show Manipulator Tool** on the left screen to activate the manipulator handler. Drag the middle handler to bend the curtain wall.

12. Rotate the bend handle 90 degrees along **Y** axis to bend the curtain wall to a curved wall.

13. Drag each of the three handles to see how they affect the bending result.

14. Apply a **twist** deformation by using the **Create Deformers > Nonlinear > Twist** tool. Drag to rotate two circular handles. Be aware that when deleting the deformer, the geometry goes back to its previous status. If deleting the history, all the deformation changes would be embedded into the geometry.

15. Apply a **lattice** deformation. Select the entire group and apply the **Lattice** tool from the **Create Deformers** menu. In the **ffd_latticeshape** node in the **History** channel on the right side of the screen, change **S, T, and V divisions** to 5, 3, and 5. Now the designer should have more control points to manipulate the lattice system.

16. Right click the lattice and select **Control points** in the popup menu. Select a group of control points and manipulate them by Move, Rotate and Scale tools. Observe how the control points deform the geometry.

17. Delete all objects' history by using the **Edit > Delete All by Type > History** menu. All the deformation results are embedded into the geometry. Select the group node, make duplication and change its **Scale Y** to -1. A negative **Scale Y** value generates a mirrored group. Now a new curved curtain wall is created.

10.4.1 Step 12

10.4.1 Step 14

10.4.1 Step 15

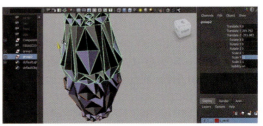

10.4.1 Step 17

IN AND OUT

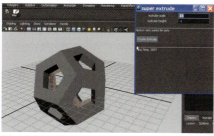

10.4.2 Step 2

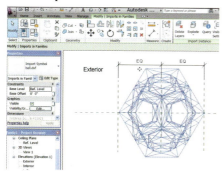

10.4.2 Step 6

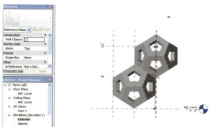

10.4.2 Step 7

10.4.2 Step 8

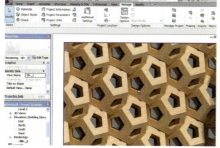

10.4.2 Step 10

10.4.2 Tutorial: From Maya to Revit

This tutorial demonstrates how to create a platonic polygon model in Maya and then use it in Revit to assemble a curtain wall.

1. Create a platonic model in Maya by using the **Create > Polygon Primitives > Platonic Solids** tool from the menu.

2. In the **polyPlatonicSolids1** node in the **INPUTS** node, set **Radius** to 5. Use Super Extrude MEL script to create a frame structure.

3. Select the platonic object, use the **File > Export Selection** menu to export it as a DXF_DCE file.

   Tip: The designer can also export the object as FBX format and then use the free **Autodesk FBX Converter** program to convert the FBX file into DXF format.

4. In Revit, create a new **Revit Family Curtain Wall Panel**.

5. Go to Revit **Insert** tag. Choose **Import CAD** to insert the DXF file.

6. Scale the imported platonic object to 5' by 5' based on the reference lines in the **Exterior view**. Save the Revit family file.

7. To create a seamless platonic wall, duplicate the platonic object and align them to a 7' high reference line.

8. Load the Revit family to a Revit project and populate the curtain wall. The platonic panels will generate a continuous pattern.

9. Customize the materials imported from Maya with Revit materials.

10. Render the perspective view in Revit.

IN AND OUT

10.4.3 Tutorial: Export geometry and vertex color from Maya to Rhino

1. Create a flat polygon plane in Maya. Set **U** and **V division** values to 10 by 10.

2. Use the **Edit Mesh > Cut Face Tool** to slice the plane with several random angles.

3. Use the **Chamfer** tool to change the plane's tessellation to a complex pattern.

4. Use the **Soft Manipulation Tool** to modify the plane into a 3-D surface. Delete the history.

5. Use the **Color > Paint Vertex Color Tool** in the **Polygons** menu group to add some vertex colors.

6. In the **Paint Vertex Color Tool** panel, use the **Import** button to select a map and apply it to the polygon. As the result, the pixel-based colors are converted into vertex-based colors.

7. Export the polygon mesh as an FBX file into Rhino. Use Grasshopper plug-ins to manipulate the geometry based on its vertex color. The RGB values of each vertex can be extracted and used to control various operations in Grasshopper.

8. To create variations across the polygon mesh, each face can be operated independently according to its vertex color.

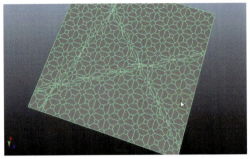
10.4.3 Step 3

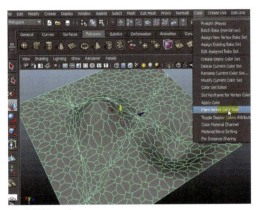
10.4.3 Step 4

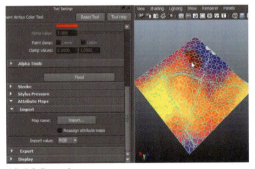
10.4.3 Step 6

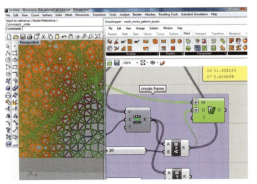
10.4.3 Step 7

10.4.3 Step 9

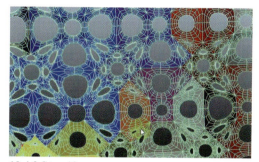

10.4.3 Step 10

9. Transfer the Rhino model back to Maya as a FBX file.

10. Manipulate the imported mesh in Maya. Use the **Edit Mesh > Merge** tool to combine vertices and the **Mesh > Smooth** tool to smooth the model.

IN AND OUT

NOTES

Chapter 1

1   Wikipedia. http://en.wikipedia.org/wiki/Parameter

2   Anderson, J., Tang, M. *Interactive information model for digital fabricator*. ARCC-EAAE 2010 Conference. Washington. D.C. 2010

3   Tang, M., Anderson, J., Aksamija, A., Hodge, M. *Performance-based generative design: An investigation of the parametric nature of architecture*. 100th ACSA Conference. Boston, Massachusetts. 2012.

4   Oxman, R., 2009. *Performance-based design: Current practices and research issues*, International Journal of Architectural Computing, Vol. 6, No. 1, pp. 1-17.

5   Aksamija, A., and Mallasi, Z., 2010. *Building performance predictions: How simulations can improve design decisions*, Perkins+Will Research Journal, Vol. 2, No. 2, pp. 7-32.

6   For each panel in the curtain wall system, designers can define parameters to respond to either 2-D bitmap inputs or a single point attractor interactively. By linking the 2-D bitmap to each panel's morphing weight, the building performance data such as acoustic and solar radiation analysis can be integrated into the design of the curtain wall system.

7   Maya was originally named *Alias Wavefront Maya*, developed by Alias Research, Inc. Maya 1.0 was released in 1998. Maya was bought by Autodesk in 2005.

8   "Each node can receive, hold, and provide information by means of attributes. A node's attributes can connect to the attributes of other nodes, thus forming the web of nodes….In short, underlying everything you do in Maya lies Maya's dynamic, node-based architecture." (Autodesk Maya Online Help, http://download.autodesk.com/us/maya/2010help/index.html)

9   Dependency graph is a visual representation of a Maya scene. Designers can use Maya Hypergraph window to view the dependency graph and connected nodes.

10   Gaudi studied the catenary arches by building a hand-crafted prototype with hanging cables. Frei Otto developed the thread wool prototype to experiment how threads were bundled by the surface tension of the water in 1958. The method can be used to create the minimal path system.

11   The fundamental shapes, such as spheres, cones, cubes, planes, and toruses are called *primitives*. Primitives are simple mathematical shapes that can be modified and expanded into other shapes. Almost everything can be constructed by starting from primitives.

12   The camera movement and motion usually include Zoom, Pan, Tilt, and Dolly.

Zoom: The camera's lens is adjusted to increase or decrease the camera's field of view, magnifying a portion of the scene without moving the camera.

Pan: The camera rotates from side to side. The camera does not change its location during a pan.

NOTES

Tilt: The camera rotates to aim upward or downward, without changing the position where the camera is mounted.

Dolly: The camera's actual position changes, such as to move toward subject during the shot.

13 Duplication will affect the object's history INPUTS node. For instance, a circle node has an INPUTS node including radius, level, and subdivision attributes. When using the default duplication, Maya ignores all INPUTS nodes and attributes. It only duplicates the final circle without the history. The solution is to turn on the duplication history in the duplicate special tool, so the new duplicated object will include all the INPUTS nodes with attributes.

14 Boolean operation creates models by adding and subtracting shapes in a variety of ways. The most common Boolean operation includes Union, Intersection, and Difference.

15 It is important to understand that the object manipulation pivot point is not always the geometric centroid of the object. When designers build a new object by Boolean operation, or other actions such as loft, revolve, or trim, the pivot point of final object can be away from the centroid. Designers can use the Center Pivot tool from the Modify menu to snap the pivot back to the centroid. Designers can also manually move the pivot point by activating the pivot manipulator using the Insert key in the keyboard, and then move the pivot with move handles. This technique is useful when rotating a door or a window based on the hinge rather than its centroid.

16 The amount of beveling can be controlled by the distance, radius, or angle value between the edges that are beveled.

Chapter 2

1 In fact, Maya actually tessellates all NURBS surfaces into a polygon mesh during the rendering process.

2 Designers must clean up illegal polygon faces by using Weld and Clean up tools in Maya.

3 Polygon Boolean operations include Union, Subtract, and Intersect.

4 The INPUTS history node contains all operations applied to an object. By deleting the history node, designers can compress the history node into the current object.

5 The Super Extrude MEL script will be discussed in Chapter 9.

6 In Rhino program, if designers convert a mesh into a surface, Rhino will break apart the mesh model into individual faces and convert each of them into a NURBS surface. This process is problematic because a simple mesh model could end up with many small NURBS surfaces. An alternative method is to slice the polygon mesh model into a series of curves and loft them into a single surface. The same logic can be applied in Maya as well.

7 This process is problematic since it will break apart a polygon model into series of NURBS surfaces. It is the same issue as Rhino mesh to the surface conversion tool.

8 Designers can either select polygon edges manually, or double click to select the edge loops. Designers can also use Project Curve on mesh to generate curves and then loft them. However, both methods will lose the accuracy of the polygon mesh model.

Chapter 3

1 As the foundation of analytic geometry, Cartesian coordination defines the position of a point by projecting the point onto three perpendicular axes. UVW defines points on the surface of the object. UVW mapping is commonly used to map textures across a surface.

Chapter 4

1 Designers can connect one joint to another joint in a skeleton. The parent joint's rotation controls the rotation of its child joints. However, the child joints' rotation does not affect the parent joint because they are in the lower hierarchy.

2 Theo Jansen's walking sculpture uses a spine and a network of rods to mimic the animal's walking legs.

Chapter 5

1 Agent based modeling simulates the interactions of multiple agents to represent a larger system. It can be used to simulate organizational behavior.

2 "A performance-based design process can be integrated with various generative and parametric design methods. Many architects have employed methods such as decision trees and rule based systems as means of solving design problems.

Some of the emerging aspects in contemporary architecture include the utilization of genetic algorithms in the design process, as well as the use of simulations and performance-driven design approaches to generate complex building forms that respond to environmental criteria." (Tang, M., Aksamija, A., Anderson, J.,Hodge, M. *Data driven transmutation: An investigation of performance based design and adaptive systems*. AIA Forward Journal 112. 2012. pp.97-104.)

3   Genetic algorithm is an optimization method that uses techniques inspired by natural evolution, such as inheritance, mutation, selection, and crossover.

4   Cellular automation is a model consisted of a grid of cells. The cells are updated by fixed rules that determine the state of each cell in each generation.

5   L-system (Lindenmayer system) is a model consisted of a string of symbols that can be expanded based on production rules. L-system can be used to generate plant growth and self-similar fractal systems.

6   Designers can create a passive object from a polygon mesh and interact with nCloth, nParticles, or nHair in the same Maya Nucleus solver.

7   Maya creates links between neighboring particles. Cross links will be automatically added for non-triangulated meshes. Links will affect the Stretch and Compression resistance of nCloth.

8   A mesh object can be set as Passive Collider within a Nucleus system.

9   With the FBX file format, designers can exchange animation data between multiple Autodesk programs such as Maya and 3dsMax. The Autodesk FBX is not designed to transfer particle data. However, it can transfer the skeleton system and standard key-framed animation across multiple programs.

10   For example, Real Flow fluid or Rhino model driven by the animated Grasshopper slider can be baked into a sequence of OBJ files. Then designers can load these OBJ files as a sequence in other animation programs such as 3dsMax and Maya, similar as loading an image sequence in video editing programs.

Chapter 6

1   When the camera is moved close to an object, there is a broader view of the background and the space seems larger. The scene will look different if the camera is positioned far away from the subject, even if a big zoom is applied to produce the same frame as the close-up shot. Rendering a close-up from distance will compress the space and reduce the depth, resulting in a flattened perspective.

2   Normal looking shots of most scenes will be the ones taken by the camera at the height of eye-level. Moving the camera to different heights can create other angles that can be used to produce special effects.

3   Designers can control the brightness or multiplier settings of a light by adjusting its intensity value. Some programs also have global or grouped lighting control. The intensity of light diminishes as distance from the light increases. The quality of shadows in a rendering can be crucial to the realism of a scene. Shadow can define spatial relationship. By casting shadows on the ground, the objects' relative positions and their relationship between each other can be easily understood.

4   A popular way to illuminate an object is to render it with a classic lighting scheme called *three-point lighting* that includes the key light, fill light, and back light. The key light shines directly upon the object and serves as the principal illuminator. The intensity, color, and angle of a key light often determine the shot's overall lighting effect. The fill light also shines on the object, but from a side angle relative to the key light. It balances the key light by illuminating shaded surfaces. The fill light also adds a matching tone to both the cast shadow and the side of the object that is unlit. The back light shines on the object from behind. It gives the object a rim of light, serving to separate the object from the background.

5   A small or distant light source, such as the sun, casts crisp shadows, while a large light source, such as the sky or a panel of lights, casts soft shadows.

6   Render nodes are various components to build a rendering. Material nodes include Blinn, Phong, Lambert, and other surface materials, as well as volumetric materials and displacement materials. Texture nodes include 2-D textures (file texture node and procedural texture), 3-D textures, and environment textures.

7   Mental Ray renderer offers photorealistic rendering for Maya. It includes various special shaders such as Ambient Occlusion. Procedural

NOTES

textures are generated with mathematical functions. They have unlimited resolution.

8   Tiling an image creates textures by repeating an image in a grid pattern.

9   A common mistake in texture mapping is to create an image with extreme high resolution, which will increase the rendering time without significantly improving the texture quality. For instance, a typical 800 pixel by 600 pixel brick image works better with tiled walls than an 8000 by 6000 pixel version of the same brick image.

10   Replacing a 3-D object with an image mapped onto a special plane is called *bill boarding*. It can save memory and rendering time. For example, a 3-D tree can be replaced by a flat 2-D bill board tree to speed up rendering.

11   TGA is a popular format used in video-editing software. It supports alpha channel. TIFF, standing for Tagged Image File Format, is a popular file format used in production software. TIFF format has 8-bit and 16-bit versions for color per channel definition. It preserves detailed grayscale information that is fundamental for generating high quality halftones used in graphic arts. An alpha channel is commonly used to support multiple layer composting because it contains a black-and-white image that masks parts of the image. Alpha channel makes it possible to select a portion of the image to be composted as foreground elements layered on top of a background.

12   Ambient occlusion rendering time can be affected by manipulating the sample level parameter. It controls how many samples the computer needs to calculate to determine the gray color value of a pixel in the final rendering pass.

13   The basic idea of image mapping is to take a 2-D image and project it onto the surface of an object.

14   As one of the most advanced and accurate rendering methods, ray tracing calculates every light ray in the scene. Ray tracing can produce images with accurate reflections, refractions, and shadows.

15   Global illumination (GI) can create images that are more accurate than other rendering techniques because it calculates indirect illumination on objects, including diffuse, glossy, and specula inter-reflection between surfaces and transmission of light from other objects, all of which closely simulate light behavior in the physical world. Photon maps are collections of small energy packets that are emitted into the scene to represent the way light travels through space.

Chapter 7

1   By rendering an animation from a virtual camera, designers can experience the building's spatial relationship before it is actually constructed. In this type of fly-through animations, the technique of motion path is especially useful for laying out complex camera movements. A 3-D motion path is easy to work with as it allows designers to define the translations and rotations of the camera in a quick way. Motion path animation is defined in several steps. It starts with a curve drawn in the 3-D space. A camera is selected and linked to the path afterwards. Then time parameters of the path are defined.

2   By animating positions and attributes of the lights using 3-D programs, designers can simulate natural and artificial lighting effects. A scene illuminated by a light that is consistently changing its color, intensity, and position, can be rendered into a sequence of still images and compiled into an animation to simulate its dynamic lighting environment.

3   Transformation attributes include Translate X, Y, Z, Rotation X, Y, Z, and Scale X, Y, Z.

Chapter 8

1   Designers are often left with design concepts that are difficult or almost impossible to be implemented in the physical world. The disconnection between digital representation methods and the real construction principles has been intensified with the rapid development of digital computation in the past decade. The freedom of digital form-making can easily be confronted by the reality of material properties.

2   For instance, Grasshopper attractors or image samplers can be used to control the radius of an array of circles parametrically. The pattern can be fed into laser cutter or CNC machine to create perforated panels.

3   A vector image is defined with mathematical expressions.

4   Maya can generate a waffle structure with an MEL script or a manual process. A Maya NURBS surface can be transferred to Rhino as IGES format. There are several methods to create a waffle form

in Rhino using Grasshopper plug-in.

5   The Unroll command in Rhino only works for a ruled surface that can be formed by sweeping a moving straight line.

6   Although twisted, hexagonal boxes can be unrolled individually in Rhino with the Unroll command. Designers can also unfold faceted polygon models with a third party software such as Pepakura. The Maya polygon model can be transferred into Pepakura with OBJ format. Pepakura automatically breaks apart the model with seams, unfolds the polygon model along the seams and transforms it into 2-D patterns.

7   In vacuum forming, a sheet of plastic is heated and stretched against a single-surface mold. The plastic sheet is formed into a permanent shape by applying a vacuum between the mold surface and the sheet.

8   Naked edges are edges along the seams of a surface. In a closed surface model, all surface normals should point to the exterior space. If a few surface normals are pointing toward the interior void, designers must flip these reversed normals.

9   Maya displacement map changes the topology of an object by moving an object's vertices according to the Alpha Gain value in the 2-D map. Different from the bump map, Maya displacement map changes the geometry of the object.

Chapter 9

1   When Maya executes operations, it posts the executed scripts and other standard output including feedback messages in the upper part of the script window.

2   http://download.autodesk.com/global/docs/maya2013/en_us/

3   The shelf is a panel that stores common tools and shortcuts in Maya. Shelf Editor allows designers to edit icon labels, names, and images.

4   The similar nonlinear approach can be realized by other tools such as WeaveBird in Grasshopper.

Chapter 10

1   The file formats used for transferring the geometric information among modeling programs are called *universal file formats*, which includes DWG, DXF, IGES, FBX, OBJ, 3DS, and SAT.

NOTES

PROJECT CREDITS

The Liquid Glacial

Architect: Zaha Hadid Architects

Design: Zaha Hadid, Patrik Schumacher

Design Team: Fulvio Wirz, Mariagrazia Lanza, Maha Kutay, Woody Yao

Embryological House

Greg Lynn FORM: Andreas Fröch, Nicole Robertson, David Chow, Jackilin Bloom, David Erdman, Jefferson Ellinger, Sven Neumann.

Photography: Martin Rand, Venice, CA

Consultants: Garden design: Jeffrey Kipnis

H2 House

Architectural design:

Greg Lynn FORM, Los Angeles, CA: Andreas Froech (Lead Designer), Jefferson Ellinger, Kim Holden, Ulrika Karlsson, Gregg Pasquarelli, Heather Roberge, Cindy Wilson

Michael McInturf Architects, Cincinnati, OH: Michael McInturf, (Design Principal), Phil Anzalone, Stephanie Bayard

Treberspurg and Partner, Vienna, Austria: Architekt D.I. Dr. Martin Treberspurg (Design Principal), Andrew Whiteside (Project Manager)

Structural Engineering: D.I.Dr. Richard Fritze

Mechanical Engineering: Dr. Peter Schuetz

Mechanical Engineering H2/Solar Components:

SIEMENS AG Austria, Ing. Franz Daberger, D.I. Michael Friess

Landscape Design: D.I.Arch. Maria Auboeck

Audio-Visual Consultant: Boyce Nemec Designs, Andrew Smith

Model Production/Stereolithography: Institute of Manufacturing Systems, New Jersey Institute of Technology

Model Photography: Studio Schwingenschloegl

MathMorph

MadCubic: Ming Tang, Jonathon Anderson.

PROJECT CREDITS

REFERENCES

Aksamija, A., and Mallasi, Z., 2010. *Building performance predictions: How simulations can improve design decisions*, Perkins+Will Research Journal, Vol. 2, No. 2, pp. 7-32.

Oxman, R., 2009. *Performance-based design: Current practices and research issues*, International Journal of Architectural Computing, Vol. 6, No. 1, pp. 1-17.

Tang, M., Auffray, C., Lu, M. *From statistical to diagrammatic: Geo-spatial & time based data visualization through parametric modeling*. 4th annual Symposium on Simulation for Architecture and Urban Design (SimAUD). San Diego. CA. 2013.

Tang, M., Anderson, J., Aksamija, A., Hodge, M. *Performance-based generative design: An investigation of the parametric nature of architecture*. 100th ACSA Conference. Boston, Massachusetts. 2012.

Tang, M., Vera, M., Anderson, J. Yeshayahu, S. *Adaptive skin: Performance driven design and fabrication*. 2012 National Conference on the Beginning Design Student (NCBDS), College Park, PA.

Vera, M, Anderson, J., Tang, M., Yeshayahu, S. *In-form: Towards a design science revolution*. 2012 National Conference on the Beginning Design Student (NCBDS), College Park, PA.

Aksamija, A., Snapp T., Hodge, M., Tang, M. *Re-skinning: Performance-based design and fabrication of building facade components: Design

computing, analytics and prototyping*. Perkins + Will Research Journal. Vol. 04.02. 2012.

Tang, M. *Visualizing GIS information: Digital fabrication and 3D diagrammatic urban models*. Assemble. d3 publications. ISBN: 0615652700. 2012.

Tang, M., Aksamija, A., Anderson, J.,Hodge, M. *Data driven transmutation: An investigation of performance based design and adaptive systems*. AIA Forward Journal 112. 2012. pp. 97-104.

Tang, M., Aksamija, A., Hodge, M., Anderson, J. *Performance-driven design and prototyping: Design computation and fabrication*. Perkins + Will Research Journal. 2011 Vol.03.02.

Tang, M., Anderson, J. *Information urbanism: Parametric urbanism in junction with GIS data processing & fabrication*. 2011 Annual Architectural Research Centers Consortium (ARCC) Spring Research Conference. Detroit, MI.

Anderson, J., Tang, M. *Form follows parameters: Parametric modeling for fabrication and manufacturing processes*. 16th International Conference of the Association for Computer-Aided Architectural Design Research in Asia (CAADRIA). Newcastle, Australia. 2011.

Tang, M., Vera, M., Anderson, J. *Representation and Realizing: a hybrid process of immaterial and material*. 2011 National Conference on the Beginning Design Student (NCBDS), Lincoln, Nebraska.

REFERENCES

Anderson, J., Tang, M., Vera, M, Yeshayahu, S. *Parametric thinking [not modeling] as a generator.* 2011 National Conference on the Beginning Design Student (NCBDS), Lincoln, Nebraska.

Vera, M, Anderson, J., Tang, M., Yeshayahu, S. *Re-tooling the logic of design.* 2011 National Conference on the Beginning Design Student (NCBDS), Lincoln, Nebraska.

Tang, M., Anderson, J. *Mathematically driven forms and digital tectonic: A formula for realizing the digital.* ACADIA 2010 conference. New York.

Anderson, J., Tang, M. *Interactive information model for digital fabricator.* ARCC-EAAE 2010 Conference. Washington. D.C.

Tang, M. *City generator: GIS driven genetic evolution in urban simulation*, Proceeding of the 96th ACSA Conference.2008.

INDEX

3-D print 150, 157

A

Algorithm 16, 19, 95,

Alpha channel 114,120, 128, 130, 135, 171,178, 194

Ambient occlusion 121, 130

Animation pass 65,

Attractor 70

Attribute Channel 39, 71

B

Bevel 40, 122, 192

Blend 67, 79, 89, 144, 186,

Blend Shape 35, 60, 67, 77,

Boolean operation 40, 50, 192

BUMP map 119, 195

C

Camera lens 111

Cartesian coordination system 64, 192

Catenary 37, 191

Center Pivot 40, 56, 185, 192

Centroid 42, 53, 56, 71, 77, 192

Chamfer 41, 44, 53, 61

CNC 18, 150, 155

Collision 37, 95, 96, 97,145

Combine 67, 68, 116

Control vertices (CVs) 49, 139

Cut Face 50, 55, 169, 188

Cylindrical projection 128

D

Deformation 59, 89, 144, 151, 159, 186

Deformer 31, 50, 59, 61, 67, 77, 82, 106, 139, 144, 186,

Dependency graph 36, 191

Depth map shadow 113, 114

Driven Key 69, 70, 71, 77

Duplicate Special 78, 89, 192

E

Edge 6, 39, 40, 42, 48, 50, 57, 106

INDEX

EP Curve 91,106, 148

Export 41, 117, 151, 154, 155, 162, 182, 185,187,188

Extrude 42, 43, 44, 45, 54, 57, 58, 79,104, 166

F

Fabrication 150, 158,

Face 39, 42, 43,44, 48, 50, 55, 57, 77, 106, 126,

Falloff Radius 41, 56, 144

Folded paneling system 71

Frei Otto 37, 95, 191

G

Gaudi 37, 95, 96, 191

Genetic evolution theory 66

Genotype 66, 73, 179

Grasshopper 97, 115, 117, 188, 193

Gravity 37, 95, 96, 104, 145,

Group 39, 88, 185

H

History INPUTS node 36, 42, 50, 125, 144, 166, 192,

I

Image sampling 171, 177

Import 182, 185, 187, 188

Incandescence channel 121, 131

Inverse kinematics (IK) Handle 88

J

Joint 82, 88, 89, 90, 192

K

Keep Face Together 43, 167

Key frame 64, 146,

L

Laser cutter 18, 151

Linear Bend Deformer 67

Loft 36, 49, 52, 148, 192

M

Mathmorph 158

Maya dynamics 96

Maya nDynamics 96

MEL script 52, 54, 58, 77, 152, 164, 166, 177

Morphing 18, 64, 65, 66, 68, 70, 72, 138, 144, 148, 156, 191

Motion Path 90, 138, 144, 147, 194

N

nCloth 96, 97, 104, 105, 106, 145, 193

nHair 96, 98, 104, 193

Non-linear 18, 30

Normal direction 55, 57, 119, 157,

nParticles 96, 97, 104, 193

Nucleus system 96, 104, 105,106, 193

NURBS modeling 48, 49, 50,

O

Outliner window 78, 88, 89, 90, 107, 146, 161, 162,

P

Parameter 16, 36, 191

Parent 17, 66, 74, 82, 88, 91, 144, 192

Parent-children relationship 82

Particle System 97, 104, 132

Performance 16, 18, 37, 94, 95, 115, 191, 192, 193

Performance Based Design 18, 37, 94, 192, 193

Phenotype 31, 66, 74, 75

Physics engine 37

Planar projection 123, 124, 127

Poke Face 42, 50, 53, 54, 58, 77, 151

Polygon modeling 43, 48, 50, 67

Primitive 21, 39, 187, 191

Projection 111, 119, 123, 124, 125, 126, 127, 177

R

Ramp color 122

Ray-traced shadow 113, 114

Revit 182, 185, 187

Revolve 107, 192

RGB values 64, 71, 122, 188

Rhino 52, 97, 115, 117, 152, 154, 155, 159, 182, 184, 188, 192, 194

S

Script 117, 152, 164, 165, 195

Script Editor 54, 164

Select Using Constraints 44

Separate 68, 193

Shader 59, 114, 118, 119, 122, 127, 130, 131, 136, 171, 182, 185, 193,

Simulated physics (Physics simulation) 19, 95

Simulation 18, 20, 35, 94, 95, 96, 97, 98, 104, 106, 145, 154, 182

Skeleton 82, 87, 88, 89, 90, 192

Skinning 82

Smooth 40, 55, 89, 117, 166, 189

Soft edge shader 122

Soft manipulation 50, 144, 154, 188

Soft Selection 41, 42, 56

Spherical projection 124

Split Face 50

Subdivision 40, 49, 89, 165

Subdivision modeling 48

Super Extrude 52, 54, 61, 79, 152, 166

T

Tessellation 44, 50, 52, 53, 97, 122, 151, 152, 166, 188

Time Slider 104, 146, 148

Tool path 155, 161

Transformation Attributes 40, 42, 82, 139, 146, 161, 194

Transparency 64, 118, 119, 120, 128, 185

Triangulate 16, 58, 193

U

U and V coordinate (UV coordinate) 49

U and V values (UV values) 49, 172

UV projection 119, 124

V

Variable 16, 164, 166, 167

Vector rendering 132, 136

Vertex 39, 41, 49, 50, 64, 97, 124

Vertex color 65, 114, 115, 116, 122, 177, 182, 188

W

Weight slider 65

Weight value 65, 70, 71, 78

Wind 94, 105

Wool thread pattern 37

Wrap Deformation 59, 61